JESUS GOES TO HOLLYWOOD

A Memoir Of Madness

Tom Matte

Jesus Goes To Hollywood
Copyright © 2020 by Tom Matte.

All rights reserved. Printed in the United States of America. No part of this book may be used or reproduced in any manner whatsoever without written permission except in the case of brief quotations em- bodied in critical articles or reviews.

I have tried to recreate events, locales and conversations from my memories of them. In order to maintain their anonymity in some instances I have changed the names of individuals and places, I may have changed some identifying characteristics and details such as physical properties, occupations and places of residence.

For information contact :
tom@madnessmathandmarketing.com

Book and Cover design by Ballyhoo Design
Book Editor : Jim Auchmutey

ISBN : 9798635940334

First Edition: May 2020

10 9 8 7 6 5 4 3 2 1

For Christie, Austin and Carson

INTRODUCTION

In *Jesus Goes to Hollywood: A Memoir of Madness*, Tom Matte tells us his sister, Robin, used her intelligence to keep her out of trouble, whereas he used his charm. I've known Tom since he was fifteen years old and can attest to that charm. He had a charisma that worked with adults, peers, children, and small dogs. But charm is a complicated skill. It requires great powers of psychic observation, the ability to analyze feedback, and a fluidity in responding with alternative reactions, all of this in warp speed. It is not a skill possessed by many people. However, in Tom's case, his behavior during his "lost years" seems to have vacillated between skill and psychosis worthy of an Oscar nomination. *Jesus Goes to Hollywood: A Memoir of Madness* demonstrates skill and charm, but a whole lot of scallywagging brain chemistry.

Advances in the study of the brain leave us breathless. This amazing organ orders our physical functions and modulates our emotions and thought processes. When all goes well, it is a marvel. When it malfunctions, it troubles not only the owner but those who love him, those who work with him, his neighbors and sometimes strangers who are just minding their own business.

I am the Father Ed who in this book Tom erroneously credits with saving his life. It is a lovely accolade I wish I could own. In truth, it was a couple of well-chosen meds, some good luck, and most importantly his own indomitable spirit that brought him back from the abyss. And indeed he was out on a psychotic limb gnawing it to bits by bad choices, fueled by disordered visions and perceptions. Apart from the psychobabble, his brain went rogue.

A man of talent, good looks and ability, successful with his family and his business, supported by good friends and living well by any measure, destroyed everything and almost everyone. He then rebuilt his life with greater insight, a healthy fear of going back, and a desire to share his "misadventures" with others.

If you read between the lines, his actions before, after and even during define courage and hope. As a clinician myself, I hope the reader will come away with a sense that no matter how dark it becomes there can be an illumination. It doesn't always happen, but it can. I believe that is the whole point of *Jesus Goes to Hollywood: A Memoir of Madness*.

Enjoy a good read.

The Rev. Edward G. Lambro, PhD, CCMHC

Our Life

Chapter 1

December 2011

I'm about to set my house on fire.

Our wooden deck seems the most logical place to start. I've got a container filled with a few gallons of gas stored in the garage somewhere. We purchased it the same day we bought an emergency portable generator for our home. It's been sitting in the garage for the past two years waiting. Waiting for its chance to fuel the generator. I've got bigger plans for it. Much bigger. I'm going to use it as a catalyst to burn my entire house to the ground.

The family has left me alone for a few days. They say I'm acting strange. I all but ruined Christmas. They left the day after to go see my wife's father in Virginia. It's good that no one is here. I don't want anyone to get hurt. I just want the house to burn to the ground and take all the lies with it. I've had enough. A person can take only so much before they snap, and I've taken all I can take.

When you think about how crazy the holidays can get, you don't typically think about burning down the house. That's madness! Crazy for the holidays means hectic shopping malls and impatient drivers looking for parking spaces. It usually doesn't involve setting the house on fire to get to the bottom of a government conspiracy that your wife is somehow involved with.

If everything goes as planned, my home will be in a full blaze in less than an hour. There will be local news helicopters overhead. Fire trucks will be lined up and down both sides of the street. And it will get prime-time coverage on all the major news networks. When the rest of the media find out what's going on inside, the coverage will go from coast to coast.

I find the gasoline container next to the generator. It's heavier than I expected. I have to lug it upstairs through the house. I finally get to the upstairs kitchen. There's a door that opens onto the deck. Our deck overlooks our swimming pool, a few acres of land, and a small private lake. It's more of a pond really, but there are plenty of bass for fishing. I pour the gas onto the wooden deck and step back. The gas spills across the deck covering the wood. Some gas falls between the wooden slats onto the wicker patio furniture below. I don't have a lighter, but I do have those long wooden matches that are typically used for lighting fires in the fireplace. With a flick of my wrist, I light the match and toss it on the deck. The fire spreads fast. Within a minute half the deck is ablaze along with much of the patio furniture below. I'm mesmerized for a moment thinking about what I've just done. Not trying to burn down the house, but altering the course of my life forever.

A few things happened that triggered this decision. I mean, who sets their house on fire? You need a reason. Even if it's total bullshit, you need a reason. When you're psychotic, reality blurs with delusion. That's just how it works. It can be a terrifying and dangerous place.

Tom Matte

Let me back up and give you some information about my life. Our life, that is. At the time of my breakdown I was forty-eight years old. I had a wife, Christie, and two boys, Austin and Carson. Austin was in high school, Carson in middle school. We lived in Johns Creek, an affluent suburb north of Atlanta, Georgia. We moved here because the schools were better, the yards were bigger, and the crime was lower. We'd lived here for eleven years. In a very tiny subdivision. It wasn't really a subdivision; it was a road that ends in a cul-de-sac with only eleven houses. We were never the type of people who wanted to live in a five hundred-house neighborhood where kids come to hang all day and friends drop by unannounced. We liked our space. We were as much a part of the community as any family.

I owned a small advertising agency in Atlanta. We did a lot of business-to-business advertising. Our sweet spot was legal marketing. Not the ambulance chasers you see on TV. Our clients included some of the Top 100 law firms in the country. These are the guys that pull in $800 an hour working with Google, Facebook, and Apple. Can you imagine making $800 an hour and still being miserable? No. Then chances are you're not a lawyer at one of these firms.

From the outside looking in, I had it made. I did have it made too, except for the drugs. I have a history of drug use. Coke was my drug of choice. It helped with my Attention-Deficit/Hyperactivity Disorder. It actually calmed me down. Focused my mind. Weird. Plus, I liked the buzz. I used on and off in my thirties. Had a few years clean and then a relapse. A few more years and another relapse. I've done my fair share of rehabs. I stayed clean for most of my forties.

From 2003 to 2008, I was clean and sober. I started training for triathlons and fell in love with the sport. It took a few years, but I had a few podium finishes for my age group for Sprint Triathlons. One age group win for Olympic distance. Yeah, me. That was amazing. Every day I woke up for a race felt like Christmas. It was a gift to be able to train so hard and compete. A runner's high is real. It also worked for swimming and biking. Training for triathlons taught me that I could get high without actually getting high. I'm not going to get all New-Agey here, but something happened to my body when I pushed it to the limit. My mind too. Something good. So why did I pick up again after five years sober? Because ... drugs. Duh.

My first brush with psychosis was April 2008. A few months before the high energy, particle smashing Large Hadron Collider went online. Coincidence? I don't think so. Looking back now, it's almost like a miniature black hole was created in my brain that sucked out all my logic and reasoning.

One night, I was on coke and looking at the computer. *Christie is cheating on me.* This idea entered my head. I knew not from where it came. Not only was she cheating, she was also an escort and an adult movie star. Somehow she had been leading a double life and I was just becoming aware of it. What a fool I'd been. How was I so stupid for all those years? I confronted her. She denied it with a you're-being-ridiculous eye roll. She thought I was joking. I wasn't. It was not a bit funny. She was a lying slut who was trying to protect her reputation and client list. Fuckin' bitch!

From that moment forward, I was on a mission. I couldn't be wrong. I would sit and stare at a computer for hours. Clicking on anything that could help me find proof that my wife was cheating on me. Checking her emails. Checking her phone. I'm not a suspicious person by nature, except when I'm on coke and accuse you of cheating on me. I'm not an asshole by nature, except when I can't find any proof you're cheating on me. I'm not a psychotic fire-starter, except when I believe the delusions in my brain are true and you will not admit to them. Then it seems all bets are off.

2008 was not a good year. I continued to use on and off. When I was on coke, I was paranoid and delusional. When I was clean, things were clearer but still not right. I always had this niggling suspicion things were not OK. When I used, I wanted to get to the bottom of it. Figure this shit out. What was I trying to figure out? Didn't matter. Anything. Without drugs I felt something was missing. I was somehow disconnected. That was a new feeling for me. I don't remember feeling like that before. It was a lose-lose situation. With or without drugs.

By 2010, my former business partner realized I was out of my mind. I stayed after work almost every day and stared at the computer for hours. You know, looking for information to prove my wife was cheating. Sometimes I would take a break and look at the ceiling. Then it hit me: She had installed cameras in the vents so she could record videos for the porn empire she was running right under my nose. I called and told my partner this new revelation. He had a right to know what was going on. Unless he was in on it too. Damn it! Who can I trust? I had been asking him about Christie's infidelities over the past few months. He was losing his patience with me. I called him around midnight, I can't remember the exact time. What I do remember was him driving down to the office and praying for me. He's a good guy. Conservative Christian. Always has nice things to say about everyone. He did his best to perform an exorcism. It didn't work. A major buzz kill, though. He called his brother, an EMT, and they tried to persuade me to willingly check myself into a detox facility. I refused. He then called the cops to see if they would arrest me and force me to go. I wasn't a threat to anyone, so they wouldn't do it. Eventually he talked me into checking myself into detox. He'd had enough. He would be gone in a few months.

It was as amicable as any business breakup could be. It was also a wake-up call to stop using. I rallied my employees, the ones who stayed with me. They wanted to believe I could get and keep my shit together. Other employees left because they'd had enough of cuckoo Tom as well. I focused hard on building the agency in my vision. At that time, my ego would not allow me to fail. I used social media as a tool to build my expertise nationally in the legal marketing field. I found a voice. I had a blog. I was a thought leader. I had Twitter followers. The company had new clients. I stayed clean for eighteen months. When I picked up again, shit went south in a hurry.

I'm staring into the flames. Staring into the fire I just started. Of course I'm on drugs. I've been using on and off again since October. The drugs reignite the idea that Christie is cheating and running a porn empire. No one will believe me. My employees and family are getting worried about me. I'm only worried about getting to the truth. I am obsessed with the idea. Anyone who disagrees with me is in league with Christie. That is what I believe in my altered state. And make no mistake, I believe it with every ounce of my being. No shred of evidence or lack of evidence to the contrary will convince me. I'm paranoid too. I think I'm being watched by the government. Obviously, Christie has contacted one of her high-profile clients with connections to follow me and make sure I don't find out the truth. I'm insane by any outside measure. Inside, I'm just trying to figure this shit out.

I panic and call the fire department. They have trucks there in no time. They quickly put out the fire. They have a question for me: "How did the fire start"?

Well, Mr. Fireman, our house was robbed a few weeks ago and it's probably the same people. Apparently someone has it in for us.

"There is a cushion from this couch inside the house that was tossed onto the deck."

Well, maybe they came in the house when I was in the bedroom. Mr. Fireman is compassionate. My dad comes over and pulls him aside and they have a talk. My dad lives a few miles away and is always helping around the house and with the kids. Mr. Fireman comes back and asks a few more questions. We wrap things up and they all leave. As Mr. Fireman walks away, he glances back one last time. The look on his face is not one I'm used to seeing directed at me. It's not suspicion; it's pity. He feels sorry for me. Whatever.

My family wants me out of the house. The kids are scared and I'm acting more erratic every day. I sleep at a local hotel. I have a suspicion they want to put me in a psych ward. I have no one to trust. Everyone is in on it. Wait! I can get help from my cousin in upstate New York. There is no way Christie has got to him. I pay a limo $500 to drive me straight through. It takes all night. I check into a hotel and give my cousin a call. He is polite as can be. He lets me stay with him for a few days. I tell him Christie is a porn star and is stealing money from the company. *OK, Tom.* He gives me the same look I got from the fireman. I spend New Year's Eve at my cousin's house while they go out and have a good time. They ask if I want to go out with them. There is no way I want to go. I just need to rest. I hire a friend of his to come back to Georgia with me. We rent a car and he drives. I pay him by the day. I need him to move some boxes out of my office into storage, things I will use later in the divorce from Christie.

The first thing I do after the fifteen-hour drive is meet with a lawyer. I file for divorce. I also need them to hire a private investigator to follow Christie. Someone who can go through my office and sweep for cameras and recording devices. No problem. They can find someone. I tell them what is going on with my wife. Taping us having sex without my consent and posting the videos online. Stealing from the company. Stealing from me. They need to know everything. My lawyer doesn't yet know I'm out of my mind. He'll find out soon enough.

Chapter 2

January-February 2012

    I spend the next few days moving boxes out of my company's offices and into a storage unit. I move anything that will help me in the divorce. Boxes filled with secret corporate files that Christie has stashed away somewhere. My cousin's friend needs to get back to New York. He knows what's up and leaves after about a week. I'm hanging out at my office for much of the day. No one comes in anymore. They are all afraid of me. I'm harassing my IT guy with phone calls, accusing him of working with Christie. Surely he knows how she is managing all of this. I owe him some money, so he is more patient with me than he should have. I'm getting impatient with the lawyers. The private investigator has done nothing. Christie hires a divorce lawyer in response to my filing. The lawyers need to communicate. I see an email from her lawyer to my lawyer. Benign stuff. I lose my shit. Now I'm convinced my lawyer has been bought off. I call him and threaten to get him disbarred. I fire him. He quits. Either way, we are done.

    I check into a Days Inn. I need to get out and walk. I drive to The Forum, a shopping pavilion. It's misting outside. For some reason I walk into James Avery. They sell Christian jewelry. I have purchased a few items here in the past. Gifts for Christie and her mom. I start asking about the huge selection of jewelry with crosses on them. Gold and Silver. The sales lady takes a liking to me. We talk for a bit. I end up spending about $6,000. Rings. Bracelets. Necklaces. Sales lady tells me they have some posters with crosses on them. Would I like to take one? Yes please. In fact, if it's not much trouble, can I have five or six? No problem, sir. I did just spend six grand. She rolls up the posters and I leave.

    I meet my dealer and get some coke. I head back to the Days Inn with my drugs and crosses and posters with crosses on them. By midnight, I'm paranoid as hell. Thank God I have these posters to put up all over the room. It will keep the demons out. I wear all the jewelry. If the demons somehow get past the posters, at least they won't be able to take my soul. I lay in the middle of the bed until the first rays of sun come in the room. I feel a little better now. I check out of the hotel and find a nearby dumpster. I throw everything in a bag and throw the bag in the dumpster – the $6,000 dollars in jewelry, an unopened, shrink-wrapped MacBook air that I purchased for some reason, and a bunch of brand new clothes. This stuff is contaminated now. It has my scent on it. When the demons come back – and they will come back – it won't protect me anymore.

    I check into a Hilton. That evening Christie calls my cell phone. Apparently the garbage man was picking up trash and found my stuff. He turned it all over to the police. The police give it to Christie. I tell her it's cursed and she can keep it. She knows I'm out of my mind, but WTF Tom! She heads to James Avery and tries to return everything. It's a little scratched up so they won't take it back. Sorry, Ma'am. The sales lady remembers me. She tells Christie that it was a bit unusual for someone to purchase that amount of jewelry but not unheard of. A bit unusual? You could say that.

There is absolutely no logic to my madness. And most, if not all, is focused around accusing the person that I have loved for most of my adult life.

If you are going to understand Christie and our relationship over the next few years, how we survived, then I need to take you back to the beginning.

I met Christie when I transferred to the University of Georgia from Young Harris College back in 1983. She was a transfer student from Radford University in Virginia. We both majored in advertising. I was in the student library one afternoon and recognized her from a class we both attended earlier in the day. It was a huge class with a few hundred students. It was one of those meetings that change people's lives forever, but they don't know it at the time. We have repeated the story of how we met many times. As far as I can remember, she wanted my help with her homework. She tells it differently: I just wanted to copy her homework. Either way, it would take seven years before she would sleep with me. I don't care who you are, that's a long time to wait for sex. She was dating someone when we met. I didn't care. I asked her out anyway. I told her we could do our homework together. Instead, when I picked her up, I took her to a movie called *Breakin' 2 Electric Boogaloo*. She hated it. That could be the reason she put off sleeping with me for seven years. Payback.

After the movie, we went back to the apartment she shared with three other girls and spent the rest of the evening talking about advertising and listening to music. It was clear that we liked each other right away. She was easy to be around. We had a lot in common. I tried to make out with her that night. She was having none of it. She was head over heels for some other guy. I was cool with the rejection. At that time I thought sex was a numbers game. I wasn't the most thoughtful guy. I was also between serious girlfriends. This was before AIDS. We started doing homework assignments together. Hanging out when she wasn't spending time with her boyfriend and I wasn't out hitting on girls. We became really good friends. Just friends.

We both moved to Atlanta after graduation. She got a job buying printing for the Portman Companies, one of the premier architectural and development firms in the country. I took a job selling printing. How perfect was that? She was my first client. I had a knack for sales. My client list grew.

We decided to move in together. I was dating around and she was dating her latest boyfriend. Neither of us was interested in the other person as a boyfriend or girlfriend. We were just friends. To give you an example of just how friendly we were, Christie would occasionally find a random pair of panties in the washing machine, fold them, and lay them on my bed for me to return to the girl. I became friends with her boyfriends. We hung out. We went to clubs together. It was all good.

We hopped in the car one Friday and took off for Destin, Florida. Christie was fighting with her current boyfriend. She had long since moved on from her college beau. I just wanted to go party. Before the weekend ended, my seven-year drought was over. You might think I would say that changed everything, but it didn't. She got back with her boyfriend. I dated other girls. We had just become friends with benefits. But the benefits were distributed over time. The occasion had to be just right. We were friends first, horny second.

Eventually she got bored with her job buying printing and I got bored selling printing. We started our first company together. We were minority shareholders. The majority shareholder was Christie's latest boyfriend. It was a small creative shop. We worked there for two years. It was a great learning experience.

After two years I had learned everything I could and decided to start a design studio with a few other business associates. I knew shit was going to hit the fan when I left. I told Christie what I was doing and asked if she wanted to be a part of my new company. She declined. She was making good money and was still with her boyfriend. I reminded her that their relationship had been a bit heated lately and things could change. She wished me luck. It wasn't like I was moving to another city. We'd see each other again. I announced my plan to start my own studio. It went over as expected. I was a revenue generator for the company and he didn't want me to leave, understandably.

I was planning on working out of my home for the first three months until my new business partners left their respective companies at the end of the year. I wouldn't have to, though. Instead, I ended up working out of Christie's home for the next three months. She had been thrown out of the company because of me and our continued friendship. His loss was our gain. Christie and I, along with two other partners, started Max Productions on Labor Day weekend of 1992. We were young, hot, wealthy, and free. Turns out it was some of the best years of our lives.

Jump ahead three years. It's 1995. Christie has a house on one side of town. I have a house on the other. Most of our friends are married now. We're both thirty-one. The company is doing fine. Making money. We've found our pace, moving away from design and printing and more into full-service advertising. The first year was rough; the last two have been much smoother.

I'm in New Jersey visiting family when Christie calls me. I'm actually in the car of an old family friend, Father Ed, a priest I knew growing up in New Jersey. (He'll reappear; he's important to this story.) I'll never forget it. It was when cell phones just started becoming popular. You could take them out of your car. It was cool as hell, like the first year the iPhone came out. I ask her what's up. These calls are expensive. A few dollars a minute, more out of state.

"Why are you calling me in New Jersey?"

"I'm pregnant."

Silence. "Are you sure?"

"Yes, I took three home pregnancy tests."

I'm livid and scared. "How could you do this? You said you were on the pill! We need to figure this out when I get back to Atlanta."

I hang up. I look at Father Ed. He looks at me and says, "Congratulations. You're going to be a dad." I don't reply. I ask him to please take me to the airport, I need to get back to Atlanta and fix this situation.

Christie and I don't see each other for three weeks. She doesn't come to work. I can't handle this. I don't want to handle this. That's why we used birth control. We finally meet face to face. She tells me point blank, "I'm keeping this baby. I don't care if you want anything to do with it. Or us. I'm keeping this baby." Madonna lyrics flash through my mind. She's thought about it a lot. Obviously. I have too. "Of course I'll support you and the baby," I tell her. I can be an asshole, but not that much of an asshole.

After things calm down, we decide to move in together. We buy a house in September 1995. I'm adamant about not getting married. I tell Christie exactly what I'm thinking. If we get married now, I will feel like it's a shotgun wedding. Things are happening so fast. She agrees. I can commit to fatherhood and living together, but marriage seems insincere. Reactive. We have been friends and lovers for too long to pretend.

Now that we've made a commitment to this child, our world revolves around his arrival. I'm looking forward to the delivery as much as she is. Well maybe not as much. She has a baby growing inside her. She wants him out. It's been nine months. Enough is enough. On January 21, 1996, Austin is born. Much to the delight of the family. 1996 is a banner year. A new baby and Atlanta hosts the summer Olympic games. Business is booming and I have a new son. Jackpot!

What more could I ask for? How about a wife. By the fall of that year I realize that I have everything I want right here. Christie and I drive to Athens, Georgia, on December 29. She has no idea why we're going to Athens. I say something about a new client. I propose to her in front of the UGA Student Library – the same place Christie and I met in 1983 when she asked me for help with her homework.

She says yes.

We get married on September 20, 1997. Carson is born on July 21, 1998, exactly two and a half years to the day after Austin. We move to our Edgewater Estates address in August 2000. The same address where I will lose my mind and try to burn down the house. But first we have twelve mostly good years.

But now the Christie I married is gone. Or she never existed. I'm not sure which. I'm heartbroken and devastated. I miss the real Christie. The other Christie. The good Christie. I want to die. How is it possible that this is happening? I want to disappear. I don't shower for days. I wish I were dead, but do drugs instead. Maybe I will die in my sleep. Everything is a big lie. I love my kids and know they will miss me when I'm gone. I don't die.

It's February 2012, and I'm staying at my dad's place. He has moved into the house to help Christie. Thank God. My 79-year-old father (or Pipere, as his grandchildren call him) has been actively involved in their lives since they were born. He and my mom got divorced when I was twenty-five. My mom moved to upstate New York to live in a small town. My dad stayed in Atlanta for his job and so he could be closer his grandchildren. He's always there when we need him. He can fix anything around a home. Inside or out. He was also a wonderful babysitter when the kids were younger. Christie used to joke that she would get him in the divorce if we ever got one. He has the heart of a hundred saints. He's a good man. This experience will take a toll on him that he shouldn't have to deal with at his age.

I start dismantling computers and looking inside. I'm not sure why. I hate this kind of work. I'm not an engineer in any way, shape or fashion. It's almost like I think I can find out the contents of a computer just by looking at its parts. This is not rational. I'm not rational. But, if you met me at this time, you would think I was normal. For a short time anyway.

I'm being followed everywhere. The satellites know my every movement and they're waiting for the right time to make their move. Who is Christie's contact in government who has this much power? I need to find out. I decide to drive to Washington, D.C. I get cleaned up and head north. I continue to have conversations with Christie.

I need her to talk to our marketing clients and tell them to finish their projects with another agency. I have made up my mind that I will never go back to work. I have made a fool out of myself building this marketing company, which is actually a front for a porn empire. Christie can have it all. I don't care anymore. I am sure she has millions stashed away somewhere.

I check in to a five-star hotel in Washington – I can't remember which one. I call an old family friend who lives on the West Coast. Someone I can trust. She picks up the phone and says, "Hello, Tom." Caller ID. Immediately I know it's not her; someone has taken over her mind. I accuse her of something. She is worried about me. She calls Christie. Christie explains the situation. She asks whether the kids are OK? Yes, Christie tells her. "Well, let me know what I can do." There is nothing she can do. There is nothing anybody can do. I am out of control.

I stay in Washington for a few days. I walk around Congress. It's freezing outside and windy. I shake hands with Al Pacino in the lobby of my hotel. I don't know why he is here. I hand him my business card. The same card to the business that is a front for the porn empire. I buy a new iPhone, one that won't be tracked by the government. I get a new number too. There are some people sleeping around outside, left over from the Occupy Wall Street movement. Why am I here again? I really didn't think this through. Christie's government contacts won't talk to me anyway, even if I knew where to go. I don't of course, because there is no place to go. Nothing is going on. The crazy is all in my head.

High Life

Chapter 3

March 2012

    I decide to drive to New York City. I've made up my mind that I'm only going to stay in five-star hotels. I don't know it yet, but I have lost my ability to plan ahead. Not completely, but enough to cause some problems – more problems, I should say. The executive function area, the area in the brain that plans for things and makes goals, is not working properly. There is a subtle shift in my mind, a shift in my crazy. Now that I've decided to leave my business and Christie there is some kind of change in my brain. I don't have to spend all my time trying to find proof about Christie's business empire. I just know and I'm tired of looking. I'm not angry anymore. It's more of an acceptance. If that's what Christie chooses, then I'm not going to stand in her way any more. She can have it all. In fact, I even forgive her for doing this to me and the kids. I forgive her. I'm really sick. A new kind of psychoses takes its place. Maybe it's not new, but it's different.

I'm staying at the Plaza Hotel in Midtown Manhattan. A suite in one of the top floors. The place is plush if a bit dated. I meet a limo driver who says he can get me coke. Lucky me. I spend a week here. I really don't remember much of this time. Memory is a funny thing. Sometimes I can remember almost every detail and moment of an event and then I reach a certain point and things are unclear. I spend a lot of time alone. A lot of time. By the end of the month, I'm back in Atlanta. I talk to Christie and she tells me clients are pissed. I don't care. I also don't believe her. She says she is handing off the clients who aren't pissed to our art director. He is going to start his own business. I tell her that's a good idea. Other than Christie and the kids, no one has heard from me in months. I become a wraith. I disappear. I close down my Facebook page, never answer my phone and refuse to even look at emails. I will be gone for two years almost to the day.

Shit's about to hit the fan. I'm staying at the Intercontinental Hotel in Buckhead, next to Lenox Square, Atlanta's most prominent shopping mall. I head over to the Apple store because I have questions about my new iPhone. The guy who helps me is named Perri Minot. I can see it on his name badge. This is the first time I become aware of something my brain is doing without my consent. While I'm talking to Perri and he is helping me set up my iCloud account, another part of my brain is deconstructing his name. Minot becomes "I'm not." Perri stays Perri. So now he is telepathically telling me "I'm Not Perri." I get it now!! He wants to help me set up my phone so the satellites can't find me. (Yes, they are still tracking me. If I'm not a danger to Christie's empire then I'm at least a nuisance. The only reason Christie doesn't have me killed is because I'm the father of her children.) Only Perri and I know this of course. He is one of the good guys. He finishes setting up my phone and I leave the store feeling pretty good about things. Someone or some group is trying to help me. Who? I start tossing around possibilities in my mind.

Sunday morning, March 11. I'm up all night. I hear someone place a newspaper outside my hotel door. I grab the paper and start skimming the headlines. Within five minutes of reading a few local stories, I have come to the conclusion that Christie is having an affair with one of the cops at the Johns Creek police station. I get in my rental SUV and start driving toward Johns Creek. It's a straight shot up Peachtree Industrial Boulevard. I'm listening to *Wrecking Ball*, the new Bruce Springsteen album. I pull into our driveway and burst into the house.

Where is he? Christie is terrified and I'm pissed. I don't wait for an answer. I search the house. He's not here. He must be at the police station about a mile away from our house. I jump into the SUV and speed toward the Johns Creek police station. I pull right up to the front doors, knocking over a flagpole in the process. I jump out of the car and start banging on the doors as hard as I can. *Come out you fuckin' pussy!! You want a fight? I will fuck you up, you little bitch!* No one is coming out. WTF! I continue banging for a few more minutes.

No one is inside. It's Sunday morning. No one is here.

How do I let them know I mean business? I decide to T-bone one of the cop cars sitting in the parking lot. I turn my SUV around, take aim, and floor it. I'm guessing impact was at about 55 miles an hour. The cop car flies through the air. I back up and do it again; just to be sure they knew I was here. I drive back to my house in my now beat-up SUV and tell Christie to come outside. She looks at me and at the car. My youngest is also at the door. He knows I'm sick. They call my dad and my dad calls the cops and tells them what I did and where I'm staying.

I'm driving back toward the Intercontinental Hotel when the SUV gives out. The engine is steaming. I can't believe I made it this far. I pull into a Mexican grocery store and leave the SUV. I pay a guy $50 to drive me the last few miles. It's about 11:30, so I go into the bar and order brunch: deviled eggs. The hotel security guard informs me that I'm going to be arrested in a few minutes and could I please come with him. He puts cuffs on me and escorts me to a small room in the basement of the hotel. I never get to eat. I'm sitting quietly when a cop comes in, pats me down, and puts me in the back of his car. He also puts cuffs on me. Extra tight. He starts driving toward Johns Creek. First we have to stop and take pictures of the SUV I left at the Mexican grocery store. It's a sunny day and warm. He parks the car so my eyes are directly in the sun. He tells me the car I totaled belongs to his partner. He asks some other questions. I don't say much. We eventually get to the station.

As soon as we get inside, I'm handcuffed to a chair. The cop who picked me up at the hotel goes into the back to do the paperwork. I'm left with another officer who is very friendly. Officer Friendly. By this time word has gotten around that some crazy fuck just T-boned a cop car at the Johns Creek police station. This is an event. Shit like this doesn't happen in Johns Creek. The cops start pouring in. All these officers got dressed up on a Sunday morning and come to the station just to see me. I'm wondering which one Christie is having an affair with. I can't figure it out. They are sizing me up. What's up with this asshole? I'm doing the same. One of them would be considered good looking enough, but he doesn't appear to be that bright. Hmmm? Maybe I'm wrong about this. Much ado about nothing.

I'm starting to get hungry. They tell me I'll eat when I get to the Alpharetta jail. I'm thirsty. They get me a Dixie cup of water and pour it down my throat. They end up giving me five traffic citations. They walk me out of the Johns Creek station to a waiting cop car. Time to go to jail. I get inside. Something is not right. I know the officer driving the car! This is the same officer who came to my office in 2008 when I told my old partner about the hidden cameras in the ceiling of our advertising agency. I ask if he remembers me. He does. He gives me the same look as the fireman.

I'm not an idiot, though. This is no coincidence. My office is eighteen miles from my home. A completely different county. He tells me he transferred here about a year ago. It was closer to his home. I'm not buying it. He is here for one reason: me. They are following me by satellite, and T-boning this cop car takes my game to another level. They need to keep a closer eye on me. I keep my mouth shut. Remember, I have someone helping me too. I just don't know who yet.

I bail out of jail around 11 that night. It has been a long day. This is my first real experience with the police and jail. It won't be my last. I have no idea how bad things are going to get.

On March 14, I fly back to New York and check in to the Mark Hotel on the Upper East Side of Manhattan. Five stars. The location is perfect. It's close to Central Park and the Guggenheim Museum. Luxury stores too. I start wearing my headphones all the time. It's the first thing I do when I wake up in the morning, put on my headphones. I listen to music constantly. I've had a love affair with music since I purchased Queen's *A Night at the Opera* at the ripe old age of twelve. In high school it was Led Zeppelin, Yes, Van Halen, Bruce Springsteen. In college I would listen to any band that was introduced on MTV. Music videos were all the rage at the time. I would watch MTV for hours waiting for a favorite song. I devoured *Rolling Stone* and *Creem Magazine* to read about new artists. As I got older, work took over and I spent less time reading about my favorite bands. I lived for the mix tape.

At some point, after the boys were born, I stopped mixing tapes and started listening to the radio on the way to work in the morning. If something struck me as interesting and exciting, I would then buy the entire album. Like Kanye West's *My Beautiful Dark Twisted Fantasy* or Ryan Adams' *Gold*. At this point, I don't go out of my way to find new music. It has to find me. And when it does, it's usually not new anymore, but it's new to me.

Bottom line: Like most of us, music has been a part of my life since I was a kid. But now I don't listen to make myself feel good; I listen to make myself feel normal. I buy a thousand songs from the Apple Store. A few hundred videos as well. Mostly rap and pop music. Always Springsteen. I have to have Springsteen.

My closest companion is my iPhone. My second closest companion is coke. I meet the same limo driver from my previous trip and he hooks me up. He also chauffeurs me around when I feel like going out for a city drive. I mostly walk, though, with my headphones firmly in place. I start buying expensive clothes. I have a love for men's fashion. I go on a spending spree, the first of many.

The music starts to influence my mind. It's telling me what to do. If not telling me directly, it is certainly influencing how I think and what I think about. There is a hidden message in every song. No, it would be more accurate to say there is a message for me in every song. It goes beyond the lyrics and the music. Someone is sending me messages in the music. I'm not sure how or if I trust them. It feels different than being followed by the government satellites, but I don't really trust anyone. It feels better than being paranoid all the time. It feels good. It gives me comfort.

    Reading also has an effect on my mind. In a few years I will read how John Nash, the mathematician from the movie *A Beautiful Mind*, thought aliens were trying to communicate with him through *The New York Times*. Everything I read has some sort of subtext. I have come to the conclusion that someone from inside the government wants me to know what's going on. He is an ally. I have no idea why he wants to help me. He's the one doing this. I can only communicate with him on his shift. His shift changes from day to day. Sometimes he works through the night. He doesn't use the print edition of *The New York Times*. He's more high tech; we communicate through the dictionary on the iPhone. When I double-click on a word I'm typing, the black bar comes up: cut/copy/paste/replace/define/share.

    All I have to do is click on /define/ and we can communicate. It's brilliant. I have no idea how this technology works. It doesn't matter. I have no idea how the iPhone works either.

    It's early evening. I'm lying in the bed of the hotel listening to music, waiting for my government insider to contact me. I'm also high on coke. The idea comes to me that both J.Lo and Shakira are in the hotel bar waiting for me. They want to tell me something, but I have to meet them in person. They will be in disguise. I will know who they are but no one else will have a clue. This is exciting. I'm a fan of both artists. What could they possibly want to tell me? I shower, put on some new clothes, and hurry to the bar. I stand in the entrance and look in. The bar is small. Two women are sitting at a small table. They look nothing like J.Lo or Shakira. This must be them! Excellent makeup artists. Great job, Hollywood!

    I walk over and ask to sit down. Sure. I offer to buy them a round of drinks. Then this happens. I will never forget it. Shakira reaches out and squeezes my right hand. "We are worried about you," she says. I tell them I'm fine. She tells me that she thinks I might want to party just a bit less. Real concern. I tell her I will think about it. "OK," she says. We sit, have drinks, and talk for over an hour. I need to get back upstairs and do some more coke. I'm also pretty sure my government contact is working now. I want to read what he has to say. I actually get their phone numbers before I go. At about 2 in the morning, J.Lo sends me a picture of her and Charles Barkley, the basketball player. She is still in disguise. Charles Barkley looks like Charles Barkley.

Chapter 4

March 2012

    I leave the Armani store on Fifth Avenue. I just bought a suede jacket. The gray color is ethereal. The purchase and some coke make for a perfect high. I start walking back to the hotel, headphones in, listening to J.Lo's album Love. On the cover she has retro '80s-style hair. It reminds me of a girl I liked in high school. I notice the people around me are moving in unison. When I stop, they stop, at least the ones within a few feet of me. When I walk, they walk. I play a game on the way back to the hotel. I stop, they stop. I stretch my hands toward the sky, they stretch their hands toward the sky. Some people peel off and others replace them on the way back to the hotel. How is this possible? Why am I noticing? I might as well have fun with it.

    Halfway to the hotel, I step into a newsstand and purchase an organic cookie. I take a bite and a few crumbs fall from my mouth. I immediately look for a garbage can to spit it out. It tastes horrible. With the hotel a few blocks away, I become convinced that the girl I liked in high school is waiting for me in the lobby of the hotel. This gives me joy! I start jogging a bit. Then I'm running. How cool would that be? The perfect way to end the day. She is not waiting. Oh, well. No worries. She will be here soon enough. What are we going to do tonight? I go upstairs and get ready for a night on the town. All dressed up, I head to the lobby and wait. I get a drink in the bar and wait some more. It's about ten o'clock at night when I realize she's not coming.

I go back to my room. I purchase the video "Papi" from the Apple store. In the beginning of the video, J.Lo takes a bite of a cookie and crumbs fall from her mouth. The premise of the video is that J.Lo controls the guys through some magic power. She can make them move with her hand gestures. This is too much for me to handle. How can my real world experience be so similar to the video? Who is doing this to me? How can all these things be happening at the same time? I'm scared and confused. I'm also sad. Really sad. I'm lonely and want some company. I want to go out with the girl from high school so much. I lie on the bed and cry myself to sleep.

The next day I wake in a daze. I start thinking about the last few months and what happened yesterday. I have to get clean or nothing will ever make sense. I decide to check in to Crossroads, in Antigua, a rehab facility that Eric Clapton helped start years ago. I know about this place because it was my first serious attempt at rehab twelve years earlier. A beautiful island location for recovery. What more could I ask for? It's not cheap: $37,000 a month. It will be worth the investment. I will clean up my mind and then be able to figure out all these strange things that are happening to me. Or that I'm making happen.

I set my check-in date for March 28. I go through the intake session on the phone and wire the money. All set. I still have a few days before I leave so I might as well do as many drugs as I can before I quit. Anyone who has ever tried to quit drugs will understand this logic. I call Christie and tell her my plan for recovery. Please tell the kids I'm getting help. I miss them beyond measure. I go to the hotel bar every night as directed by the music. I have conversations with Madonna one night. Eminem another. Both in disguise of course. Some of the other patrons are also Hollywood celebrities in disguise. George Clooney. Matt Damon. My inside government contact has become conspicuously silent. Somebody must be on to him so he is keeping a low profile.

I'm scheduled to leave on an early flight the next morning. One final night of partying. I meet my dealer and head straight to the hotel bar. It's crowded. Standing room only. Just as I am about to leave, a table opens up. I sit down instead. The waitress comes over and I order a drink. Matt Damon is sitting on my immediate right. We can't help but incidentally brush against each other when we move. This is the second time he is here. Huh? The first time he was on the other side of the bar. Now he keeps hitting my elbow with his arm and apologizing. I use my hands to wave away his apology, like it's no big deal. He keeps looking at me with this devilish grin. I try to ignore him and walk away.

My headphones are on. They are always on. I'm listening to the Taio Cruz & Ludacris song "Break Your Heart." With the bar music in the background, I simply turn up the volume. I start getting a weird vibe. Something feels off. I have a sudden awareness, a terrifying realization. The Mark Hotel is a Gateway to Hell! Right here in New York City. The Devil is calling for my soul. He is toying with me. Even the name: the Mark Hotel. The Mark of the Devil!!! The sign of the beast! These are not real people. They're demons. Damon ... demon. Shit!

I need to get out of here fast. I can't make it obvious that I've figured it out or they won't let me leave. They plan on killing me tonight before I check out. They know all my plans. My flight was booked through the concierge. I finish my drink and head upstairs. I get safely to my room and head to the bathroom. I look in the mirror. More horror. My face starts changing. I'm turning into a demon too. I'm so scared that I throw the rest of the coke in the toilet. Serious fear. I need a drink to calm my nerves. I take a long swallow of vodka right out of a mini bar bottle. I sit on the bed and start praying like a motherfucker. On my knees. Please God! I'm sorry for all my sins. Don't let them take me to hell! I was born again at Bible school when I was a teenager, so I have that going for me. Somewhere I have a new cross necklace. I find it and put it around my neck. I feel better. "Although I walk through the valley of darkness I will fear no evil." The Bible verse repeats over and over in my mind.

    I stay awake all night. I start packing. It makes me feel better. It's still dark outside when the phone rings. My ride to the airport is here. I need help with my bags. They send a porter. I hear a light knock on the door. I'm afraid to open it. If I don't look him in the eyes, then maybe I'll be able to get to out of here alive. I let him in and keep my eyes averted. All the bags are lined up next to the door. I have six pieces of luggage. I've purchased a lot of clothes. The porter tries to make small talk. I ignore him.

    Outside feels great. I made it. I take a deep breath of fresh air. I swear to never do drugs again. I pace back and forth as the porter and the driver put my luggage in the trunk of the limo. The porter opens the back door for me, his right hand extended waiting for a tip. Out of habit, I reach in my pocket and hand him a wad of bills. I have no idea how much, nor do I care. As my butt touches the backseat, I make eye contact with him for the first time. He has no eyes. Instead he has two black holes where his eyes should be. He is smiling. I slam the door shut and start praying again.

The detox area at Crossroads is a bit like a hospital. Other than this, it's like a high-end Caribbean resort. Dining outside in an open gazebo. Swimming pool. A gorgeous bay view. Paradise. If you are going to get clean and sober, you could do much worse than this.

They take my iPhone and more importantly my music. Not cool. Without music in my ears, I have an uncomfortable restlessness. It's not anxiety exactly. It's hard to name. I will have to socialize with the other addicts. This isn't my first rodeo. I know the drill. My first night here happens to coincide with the admittance of a beautiful twenty-six-year-old named Starr. Her room is directly across from mine. We will both be moved into general housing in a few days. It's 2 in the morning and I'm in the Galley getting something to eat. The Galley is a small room with snacks provided 24/7. Starr walks in and introduces herself. I can't help but notice her beauty. She reminds me a little bit of Elizabeth Taylor. A little bit of Vanessa Hudgens. She can't sleep either. We start talking about drugs. She is just starting to detox from heroin. Her next few days are going to be rough. We sit in the common area and talk for a few hours.

Rehab is a manufactured setting designed to help addicts get clean, thirty days of intense education and self-reflection. No outside distractions. A by-product of this is that you build relationships with other people very quickly. If you have been to as many as I have, you also learn that someone you despise on the first day can be a friend by the second week. Someone you loathe on the first day, you admire, respect, and understand by the time they graduate.

And someone you like in the first five minutes you can really, really like in a few hours.

The next day I tell one of the many therapists that I need my headphones to relax. He tells me to bring it up with the psychiatrist when I see him. When will I see him? In a few days. Fine. I can wait a few days if I must. Starr doesn't come out of her room all day. Early that evening I get a knock on my door. Starr asks if she can come in my room and talk. Technically she is not allowed, but the nurse is doing other things. We are the only two people in detox. She sits on the end of my bed and tells me she is starting to feel like shit. She asks if I will help her later if she needs it. Of course. Just knock on my door.

Sometime later that night, she sticks her head in my room and calls my name. "Tom, are you awake?" She is really sick. "Come in my room and talk to me." She looks like hell. She is in the middle of what will be a very long detox, and her body is miserable. If that were me, I would want to be left alone. She wants me to stay and talk, something I'm more than happy to do. All of a sudden she runs to the bathroom and starts throwing up. I tell her I hope she feels better and get up to leave. "Come here please," she says. I hesitantly stick my head around the corner of the bathroom. She points to her hair and continues to puke. I'm confused for a minute, but finally figure it out. She wants me to hold her hair so she doesn't get vomit on it. I kneel down next to her and pull her hair back into a bun. I hold it until she's done. She finally gets up, crawls back in bed, and passes out. I let myself out, making sure the night nurse doesn't see me.

Chapter 5

March-April 2012

Instead of giving me my headphones, the psychiatrist writes me a prescription for my anxiety. I would rather have my music. I need my music. My iPhone is kept in a closet adjacent to the detox area. I saw them put it there when I checked in. It's in a clear plastic bin with some of my other belongings. I tell one of the nurses I need to get a number off my phone for the long-distance family session they have scheduled for me. The closet is a walk-in with shelves on both sides. He opens the door and points. I walk in and grab my phone. I ask him if I can take it around to the nurse's station so I can write down my number. He tells me to make it quick. I go through the motions of writing down the number and hustle back to the closet. Good. He is still standing there with the door open. I thank him, show him my phone, and walk inside. By my second step, I have quickly stuffed the phone down the front of my pants. My heart starts racing. I grab the plastic bin off the shelf and place my now empty right hand inside the bin. I rustle it around to make some noise. I place it back on the shelf. I turn around and walk out. Easy as pie.

I become fast friends with a fellow patient from Antigua, Shelby. He is a few years younger than me. He is a local celebrity. He had a hit song on the islands when he was younger. Most of the staff already knows him. In fact, that's how I first heard about his fame. He never brought it up. He also comes from island money with political connections. To top it off, he tells me he is a direct descendant of King Solomon. Usually when I see him he is carrying an old soft white leather-skinned Bible. It smells like ... I can't place the scent. Heaven? Whatever it is, I love it. After my run-in with the demons, I have decided to renew my faith. He lets me borrow his Bible when he's not using it. Within a few days, I'm convinced that I'm Christ resurrected.

I was raised Catholic, and religion has always been a part of my life. When I was very young, we went to church every Sunday. As I got older, my parents were more forgiving about missing church, probably because they stopped going themselves. I liked the stories from the Bible, the positive lessons from the Old and New Testaments. It was harder for me to buy into the fire and brimstone. Even at seven years old, when a nun was threatening me with eternal damnation for causing a ruckus in Sunday school, I could tell that it was for breaking her rules, not God's. My young brain couldn't wrap its head around a loving God being so uptight and kid-unfriendly. By the time I was a teenager, the only time I went to church was during mass at the private Catholic high school I attended and graduated from. Not to say that I didn't believe in God, Christ, and the resurrection. I did. I still do.

So it was puzzling to find myself an active participant in his (my) second coming. I was always taught to be Christlike. No one ever said I would actually be Christ. But you know what they say: God works in mysterious ways. What is interesting about this new revelation is that even though I believe it's true, I'm also smart enough not to tell anybody. Not yet anyway. I remember how things went down the last time I was on Earth. Some of you were not very nice to me. I need to get things sorted out before my big reveal. Over the next few days, I retrace my life story through the Bible. I'd completely forgotten the whole Lazarus miracle. Mad skills, right? It's nice to see that I had such an impact on so many of you. When I'm not reading, I spend much of my time talking with King Solomon's descendant.

I don't know it at the time, but soon enough I will realize that I don't need to be on coke to have psychotic thoughts. I have them all the time. I spend the rest of my free time secretly listening to music or talking with Starr. I also do the recovery homework. I have to be careful with the music because the battery will eventually run out and I don't have the charger. Reading the Bible is starting to give me a similar comfort to the music. Not as soothing but close enough.

Starr and I are sitting outside one evening when we notice some tiny birds eating the seeds near our feet. They don't appear to be scared. I pick up a few seeds and place them in my open palm to see if they will eat. After a short time, one of the birds snatches a seed and flies away. Starr laughs, surprised. "You're like that monk who takes care of animals."

"St Francis of Assisi you mean?"

"Yeah, that guy."

I'm really Jesus, but I don't disagree with her.

Shelby and Starr hit it off as well. The three of us spend a good bit of time together, mostly in the smoking area. I don't smoke, but it's the social hub of recovery, the place you go if you want to bullshit or find someone when they're late for a recovery class. We talk about the islands a lot. How time is different here. It's slower. More laid back. They both love St. John, a tiny island next to St. Thomas, in the U.S. Virgin Islands. Starr's family owns a bar on St. John. You can't miss it. It's the first one you come to when you get off the ferry. You have to take the ferry from St Thomas. The island is too small for a landing strip. The only way to get there is by boat. Sounds like a really cool place.

When you feel ready, you have to tell your life story to the other patients. It's a relaxed setting with everyone sitting in a big circle. There are about twenty people present when I tell mine. It's my tenth day here and it feels really good to get all this out in the open. Well most of it. No one yet knows that I'm Jesus. I keep that under wraps.

I talk about my childhood. Many addicts have a history of drug or alcohol abuse in their family. My situation was different. My parents never had addiction issues. Their parents? From some of the stories I've heard, probably. What I'm trying to say is that I never saw the damage firsthand that addiction could do to a family. My older sister and I had a very happy childhood. Robin was much quieter than me. I used my charm to get out of trouble. She used her brain to stay away from it. We had the normal big sister, little brother relationship. I bugged her, she tolerated me. We loved each other. We moved around more than most and I became a bit of a class clown to get attention and fit in, but we had it good growing up. We were solidly in the upper middle class. I went to two private schools, the first in Thorpe, England, where my dad was transferred for a year. He transferred around a good bit as a consultant for a number of insurance companies. The second was a Catholic high school in Wayne, New Jersey, where I graduated. We never wanted for anything. My dad was one of eight siblings: seven brothers and a sister. He was poor growing up. He promised himself that his kids were not going to have to go through the same financial suffering he did as a boy, and he delivered on that promise. My mom was a wordsmith who loved to write poems and children's books. She even wrote a children's book about the birth of our first son, Austin from Boston. She self-published. It wasn't a best-seller, but it's family history. She also loved to play word games. She was fun if a bit on the neurotic side. As she got older, it got worse. She was never diagnosed, but looking back, I think she had a touch of obsessive-compulsive disorder.

I talk about how I was first introduced to cocaine when I was at Young Harris College. It was the night before finals. I had three exams scheduled on the same day. All the students were either studying in their rooms or in the library. It was around 11 at night when a friend asked if I wanted to do a line of coke. He told me it would help me stay awake and study. I was preparing for B's across the board in all of my classes, so I thought, what the hell. I did a line of coke with him and went back to my room and cracked open a book. I had a borderline A grade for one of the classes and I figured it couldn't hurt to study some more. Plus, I was wide-awake with a rush from the drugs. I was also focused. With a little help from my friend, I stayed up all night studying. I ended up with two A's and a B in my classes. I made the dean's list. That was a first. The message was clear: With hard work and a little coke, I could do anything.

I didn't get addicted right away. It would take another twelve years of recreational using before I really dove in head first with the coke. It was about the same time my partners and I started our ad agency. I didn't use every day, but it did get in the way of my relationship with Christie. After the kids were born, Christie insisted I get totally clean. It worked, for a while anyway. But I had set a pattern, and after a few years I would be right back in it. It took me a few relapses to realize that I was the one who had to want it. To be clean.

I tell them about my wife's affair, the divorce, the fire, the car wreck. I still believe my soon-to-be ex-wife is privately running a porn business and my ad agency is just a front. She has powerful bosses with even more powerful government connections. As long as I don't harass her anymore, they will let me live. Christie wants me around for our kids. She hopes if I get clean I will be normal again. I hope that if I get clean I can start a new life somewhere else. We both want me clean and sober – the one thing we can agree on.

It's Saturday, April 7, 2012, the day before Easter. I'm scheduled for a personal call that evening. We are allowed forty-five minutes maximum. The phone is in a windowless room used for group sessions. The room is always locked so you need a nurse with the key to get in. I have my iPhone with me and plan on spending some time listening to music instead of making a call. It's more private than the bedroom. I don't have to worry about my roommate walking in. More importantly, Starr is going to meet me there so we can listen to music. She knows I managed to get my iPhone. She also knows we have to be stealth or I'll get in trouble. She wants to listen to Rihanna. Great, I have a few Rihanna songs.

I hear a soft knock and let Starr in the room. No one sees her come in. I've been in here fifteen minutes already, half listening to music and half waiting for a knock on the door. She sits down next to me and we share the headphones. One in my left ear and one in her right. This is the closest I've been to her since I held her hair. We listen to a few songs. I think I'm supposed to do something, but I'm not sure what. I'm getting nervous. She is giving me no indication that she is in the least bit interested in any type of physical relationship. I know this at a gut level. She has certainly given me more attention than the other patients. Of this I have no doubt. We are friends. Simple as that. But I'm really confused. Anxious. I know my time is almost up, so I suggest she leave. I don't want us to get caught. She is standing at the door about to open it when I blurt out, "Do you want to kiss?"

"What? No." She looks at me wide-eyed and heads out.

I'm left alone knowing this was stupid. Beyond stupid. I knew she would say no. I would have kissed her, but I didn't. The music was giving me mixed messages. Now I'm really confused. At least I tried. I went through the motions and said what I was supposed to say. I was sure that's what the music wanted me to do. Ugh. I can't help but feel embarrassed too. If I knew what was coming the next morning I would have tried to swim off the island.

Easter morning is beautiful. Almost everyone is at breakfast. The food is served cafeteria-style. There are long tables set up under the gazebo. Usually there's anywhere between eight and fourteen people around a table. I'm sitting next to Shelby when Starr comes in with Cassidy. Cassidy came in a few days after Starr. After detox, they started sharing a room. She is a few years younger than Starr. It's obvious that Cassidy has some issues other than drugs. We all do, but hers are sitting right at the surface waiting to explode. Today she is going to be Starr's protector. She sits at the end of our table and immediately shouts, "Guess who tried to make out with Starr last night? Guess who is hitting on girls half their age?"

Holy shit! This is really happening. I'm being called out by a twenty-two-year-old for making a pass at her roommate. Cassidy is getting off on the scene she's making. Shelby looks at me and whispers, "What the hell happened?"

My face is turning bright red. I don't know what to say. Foolishly, I thought Starr wouldn't say anything. I respond how any normal person would in this situation. I get up, tell Cassidy to shut the fuck up, and go straight to my room. I can't even look at Starr. She knows I'm pissed. Not at Cassidy but at her.

I immediately make the Christ connection. It's Easter, and I've just been publicly crucified. Never mind that Christ was crucified on Good Friday and rose from the dead on Easter Sunday. It's close enough for crazy.

Pacing in my room, I resolve to never make a pass at a woman again. So dramatic. But I mean it. I'm too old for this. I also know there is going to be hell to pay with the therapists. This is a big deal in rehab. Nothing can just happen. Everything is a big deal. If we scratch the surface, what will we find? I'll tell you what you will find: Jesus Christ. They won't see that coming. I avoid the other patients most of the day. Except Shelby. He checks in on me. He says he's surprised she turned me down. He thought she was giving me subtle hints too. Well she's not.

The next day, I'm called to the therapist's office to discuss what happened. Starr and I are ordered not to be alone together for the next few days. Not that you can ever really be alone in rehab. They are talking about alone in the smoking area, or alone before a class starts, or eating together. The therapists thought we were spending too much time together anyway. So they've been watching us. I should be used to people watching me by now. I make up my mind I've had enough of this place anyway. I need to get out of here. Something is telling me to go. I start making plans to head back to the States. The therapist also doesn't know I'm Christ. I don't tell him. In time I will learn that believing you are a prophet can be a symptom of schizophrenia. For now I just roll with it.

I'm leaving my room to go to lunch and Starr hurries up beside me. People are in front of us so we're not technically alone. She asks me to walk slower. She wants to apologize. She didn't mean for any of this to happen. In fact, it's not the first time a man misread her feelings for him. And, if she is being honest with herself, she can see how I could have done the same. She wants me to like her. I have to admit this makes me feel better. It also makes me like her more, because she's being so forthcoming. In any case, I'm tired of this place and I need to get out of here. She can't believe I'm going to leave. I promise her I am. We exchange email addresses. I tell her I'll contact her once I settle down back in the States. I'm gone the next day.

Chapter 6

April-May 2012

  I fly directly to Los Angeles and check into the Beverly Hills Hotel. I stayed here a few days back in February when I was still being followed by the government satellites. Other than that, it was pretty uneventful. However, I did meet an employee of the hotel who could get me drugs. This time I have six suitcases filled with clothes. I need help unpacking. My stuff almost doesn't fit in the closet space or the dresser drawers. As soon as I'm done unpacking, I head over to Saks Fifth Avenue. I'm looking for Jeffrey, a salesman in the men's department. We hit it off the last time I was here. He has an eye for what looks good on me. I trust his opinion. I spent a bunch of money with him on my last visit, and today I do the same thing. I also stroll around Beverly Hills picking up jewelry and other items from the various luxury stores.

  Over the past few days, I've noticed something new happening to me. I'm starting to see colors in a new way. They have become more vibrant to me. I notice different shades of the same color, subtle shades that I never would have paid attention to before. I also match colors from across a room. For example, if I'm holding a shirt in the men's department and look across the entire store, my eye will catch a tweed print that I know will work as part of an ensemble. I look across the street at another store's window display and the matching shoes immediately jump out at me. This is a curious new skill I have. I find it very puzzling. It happens all the time. I see things that might not typically go together and match them up in new ways. Why am I looking across the room anyway? What part of my brain knows I will find what I need there? If this happened in a vacuum it would be curious enough, but now that I'm Jesus it's even more odd. Why would Jesus care about men's fashion? From what I recall, Jesus typically wore a plain white robe and sandals. Boring. I purchase three rosaries from different jewelry stores in Beverly Hills. They are made of precious metals and stones. I wear them on my right hip similar to the way bikers wear chains to hold their wallets. This becomes my signature fashion accessory. I wear them almost every day. You would think, considering my past, crosses would bring up bad memories. They don't.

    It's the middle of the night and I'm restless. I decide to hire a driver who takes me to Las Vegas. His name is Sonny and he's a talker. Talks when I want to talk and talks when I need quiet. I'm OK with it, though. Las Vegas is a three-hour drive from LA. Plenty of time to get to know somebody if that's something you have a mind to do. We both share a love of history, Roman history to be specific. We start with Julius Caesar and his conquest of Gaul to the civil war and his dictatorship. We like to talk about other eras as well, but this is where we start. We arrive at sunrise. By the time we get there, I want to turn around. Instead I find a casino and decide to kill an hour. The casino is bright red. Owned by the devil, I'm sure. I actually think this. No demons in sight, though. I lose a few thousand dollars and find Sonny. We drive back to LA. Other than meeting Sonny, it's a total waste of time. Sonny doesn't know it yet, but he will perform numerous acts of kindness for me.

    I've managed to get a ticket to Coachella, the music festival, on Saturday, April 14. I'm too old to go but really don't care. I'm going to get a ride from Sonny and hang out for the night. We arrive sometime around 8; it's dark, but I want to see a few bands. No headliners. Or I should say, no one I know. He drops me off at an intersection with a few cops. There are cops everywhere. I start walking toward the sound of the stages and eventually they come in view. One of the bands is using a red screen to play behind so the effect looks like they are playing while on fire. It freaks me out. I turn and head back to my waiting car. On my way I pass an occasional demon. They ignore me. Or don't see me. It's dark as night. It is night. It's also cold. The coldest Coachella on record. Almost freezing in the desert. Temperatures are usually in the 90s. I'm lost. This is a big place, and I've somehow gotten turned around. It takes me an hour to find my ride. The only way I make it is with the help of the cops. They are there for every step. Thank God.

    I'm sitting at the bar in the Polo lounge of the Beverly Hills Hotel when a tall, elegant woman takes a seat next to mine. There's a limited eating area at the bar. She starts to make small talk about her business trip. She is dressed in a gown, which is somewhat unusual. She orders a drink and asks me what's good on the menu. I tell her the salad. She says she loves meat. Hmmm. OK. After a moment I realize her left hand is slowly changing shape. First an extra finger starts to grow next to her pinky. Then her thumb turns into a claw. Is this a demon? I look up at her face and while she is looking at the menu, blood starts leaking from her pupil into the white area of her eyes. Yeah, she's a demon. Why is she so close? She should be afraid of me. At least show some respect. I'm Jesus. Am I pre-crucified Jesus? I still have powers, right? I'm sure not going to make a scene and cast her out amongst the swine. Maybe that's what she wants. I'm curious. Partly, because I'm not terrified. I'm scared but not terrified. Not yet. She puts down the menu and asks me to join her in the other bar of the hotel. It's less crowded and we can talk. She starts to get up and I tell her I will join her in a minute. When she leaves, I close my tab and head to my room.

The room is scattered with clothes and other things I've purchased. I do some more coke and have a drink. I'm looking at the walls, and heads of demons start pushing through the wallpaper. I can see the outlines of the horns and the teeth. I'm starting to get really scared now. I need to get out of here ASAP. I mean, leave for good. I jump in the shower and think. They can't hurt me, but they can scare me. A child demon has drawn a ghost on the shower glass and written "Boo" next to it. So close. Creepy. I get out of the shower and pack. One suitcase only. I'm in fear for my life now. I have to get out. I grab my bag and head toward the valet area.

It's the middle of the night. I need a cab to the airport. It will take just a few minutes, the valet tells me. I'll wait over here. I step about twenty feet off the main valet area when I see him. A very old man is leaving the hotel the same time as I am. He is hunched over and uses a cane. He is wearing a dark gold robe. He is walking slowly, his head down, focused on his steps. He has many servants with him. He is clearly rich. His Rolls Royce pulls into the valet area. My taxi pulls in behind. I jump in the back of my cab ignoring the old man, who is not an old man and not just a demon; this is the Devil. Satan. Lucifer himself. He has many names. He is sizing me up for some test. A game for him. Life and death for me.

This is the second time I've been run out of a hotel by demons. This time I leave everything I've purchased in the room, easily $30,000 worth of clothes and jewelry. I never even check out of the hotel. Part of me is sure they will call and ask what to do with my belongings. Part of me thinks the test has already begun. Part of me is wrong.

I fly to Atlanta and check in to the Ritz-Carlton in Buckhead. I've rented an SUV for a few days. I drive by my house and check in on my kids. They see that I'm sober. Scared sober. I haven't used since that night a few nights ago. I miss them terribly. I stay for only an hour or so and promise my oldest we will have lunch tomorrow. His face lights up at this idea. When I leave the house, I head downtown to meet my dealer and score some coke. I head back to the Ritz ready to party. Alone. I'm up all night doing coke. Other drugs as well. Anything to alter my reality. I'm in mental pain all the time and I don't know how to fix it. I do know how to numb it, so that's what I do. My thoughts are not my own anymore. I'm being influenced by the music. Or reading. I don't know this yet. It will take a few years to make this connection. For now, I just act on whatever comes to mind.

It's early morning and I decide to go for a ride. To this day, I don't know why. I have no explicit instructions in my mind. A CD is playing on the stereo. I can't remember which one. I drive north of Atlanta. I'm in Hall County, Georgia, when I start driving the wrong way down the highway. I'm scared but can't help myself. I miss cars by inches. I lose a hubcap, flatten a front tire and keep going. I finally clip a car and flip my SUV. I think I'm going to die. While my car is rolling, I scream, "I'm Job. I love you, Eve." I have no idea what part of my brain that came from. It makes no logical sense. This is odd even in my crazy world. I think I'm dead, but I'm not.

I get arrested. I'm not hurt and by some miracle, neither is anyone else. The cop asks if I want to go to a hospital before I go to jail to see if there is any internal damage. Yes. I'm laying on a gurney and the doctors and nurses are all talking around me. They don't talk to me because I'm dead. My body must have been ripped to pieces in the accident. I'm scared again. I start to think I died and went to hell. I'm being punished because I thought I was Jesus. I'm not Jesus anymore and I will never be Jesus again. I will silently pray non-stop for the next seventy-two hours.

Chapter 7

April-May 2012

  The holding cell in Hall County is cold all the time. They do this on purpose. The floors look like gray ice. The holding cell is where you wait while they process you into the main jailhouse. It is not a quick process. Nothing about jail is fast. I get here at noon and don't get checked into the main cellblock until 3 the next morning. At one point, the cops bring a guy in screaming at the top of his lungs. He is wrapped in a straitjacket and being pushed on some kind of hand truck. The cops are beating the shit out of him, telling him to keep quiet. It's really fucked up. I wonder if they will do that to me. I know this is the first layer of hell.

  A guy sits next to me with fangs. By the time they start checking us into the main cellblock, there are twenty of us in a holding area designed for ten people. Half the men either stand or sit on the dirty floor. If you knock on the little glass window in the middle of the door, you may get an answer, but you won't get any help. Lunch is a bologna sandwich and cookies. Dinner is beans and weenies and a square of cornbread. I don't eat any of it because I think it's the remains of dead people cooked in the kitchen. I don't eat for two days. When you finally get checked in, they give you a large two-by-two-foot bin that holds all your jail belongings. A thin bed mattress, a sheet, a plastic cup, and a half plastic spoon. They also give you a plastic ID badge and number to track your purchases from the online store. This is a big money maker for the county. The phone calls are another huge moneymaker. Charging ridiculously high fees. It's a racket pure and simple.

    I walk into the big holding area. All the inmates feel a compelling urge to yell something stupid. It's like a zoo. I'm processed with a guy who has shown me the ropes and told me what to expect. I don't leave his side. I feel like a baby duck following his mother. There is a big common area with the beds in the back. Each bed is stacked two deep, like bunk beds. They manage to squeeze eight beds into each pod, four on each side. They have three pods upstairs and three pods downstairs. The shower areas are all the way to the left. One upstairs and one downstairs. With this kind of set-up, you can hold fifty-six inmates. There is one little TV about twenty feet off the ground. It's run by a remote control that I never see and don't care about in the least. It's 3 in the morning, so the TV is off. I find an empty bunk and lay down on my mattress. I pull the sheet over my head and drift off to sleep, exhausted.

    I stay here three miserable days. That's the rule in Hall County for a DUI – three days minimum. I also had an empty bag of coke, which brings a felony charge. I'll need a lawyer. At the courthouse a man comes over and offers his services. I hire him on the spot. He hands me his number and tells me to call him when I make bail. I bail out the night of the third day. I've never felt better in my life. Freedom. It wasn't hell. It was jail. Close, but not hell. I'm ecstatic. I have my music again! So calming. I take a cab all the way back to the Ritz-Carlton where I've still been paying for a room. The irony is not missed on me. Plush sheets. I order a huge steak from room service. I sleep like a baby. The next day I wake up and decide to go to the islands. St. John to be exact. Maybe Starr is out of rehab and went to see her family. I would love to see her. Shelby too.

Each day I was in jail was a day closer to the realization I wasn't Jesus and this wasn't Hell. This is a somewhat comforting shift in my psychosis. I don't know it at the time, but I will miss a pretrial hearing and soon have a bench warrant out for my arrest. Apparently the lawyer I hired was not one of Hall County's finest. Not by a long shot. Imagine the most incompetent person you know. Now give him a law degree. That's my lawyer.

I haven't reserved a room on the island. I'm going to wing it. Be adventurous. On the ferry ride over I have a new psychotic episode that shifts my fear away from biblical retribution over to the more pedestrian alien abduction. The ferry is crowded. I'm sitting outside near the front of the boat. The sun is behind us. There are people all around, but if I catch the angle right in the shadow, I can see the antennas coming out of these insect-like aliens. Aliens posing as people. Classic. Not all of them. Just a few sprinkled here and there amongst the tourists. Not only that, they are telepathically telling me that I will never leave the island alive. I haven't done coke all day, but that doesn't stop my mind from working overtime.

I resign myself to my fate and find a hotel. It's more of a condo with a kitchen. It's on the fourth floor and overlooks the bay. Walking distance to the small downtown tourist area. This is a new building and the phones don't work yet. My iPhone gets no service either. I only have the songs I purchased on iTunes as companionship. I can't even call Christie and tell her where I am. I decide to purchase an Island phone with twenty hours of talk time as part of the plan. I need to give her an update and check on the kids. When I get it back to the room, I can't understand the instructions. In fact, I'm starting to have trouble understanding anything. Reading is very difficult. I will read the words and understand the meaning of each word, but I can't put sentences together. I can't follow instructions of any kind. This doesn't scare me as much as it should. I know how to read, so I think it will eventually get better. My mind is somehow unraveling and I can't stop it. Thinking is becoming harder and harder. So many things begin to shift mentally while I'm on the island.

I meet a homeless guy who sleeps on the beach. His name is Hollywood. He will be my main supplier on the island, eventually becoming a friend. He gets me coke and weed. I also start to drink. A fifth of vodka every few days. This is unusual for me. I stopped drinking hard years ago. I just don't enjoy it. Here on the island I enjoy it again. The weed is also relaxing. I get really fucked up every day. I left most of my clothes at the Beverly Hills Hotel, but I purchased some new things when I was in Atlanta. I also buy a bunch of island jewelry and additional clothes. I find these two black wristbands made from Manta rays. They are made for women, but I don't care. They look good on me. I look like Spartacus. A 5-foot-6 Spartacus who weighs 150 pounds. Over the last four months my diet has gotten horrible. I eat once a day. Five hundred calories. Usually a burger. Maybe a Smoothie. A few slices of pizza. I'm the leanest I've ever been in my life. I don't exactly have a six-pack, but my stomach is flat as a board. I also carry a backpack everywhere. Filled with an extra shirt, shorts, shoes, whatever I think I might need. I stick my iPhone in the pack as well. It's only good for the music that I have on the phone. No Spotify or streaming music. No email or phone service. It's OK, though. I have a thousand-plus songs and a few hundred videos. Headphones on, my music is always playing. I walk everywhere. The island has lots of hills. Other than the downtown area, everything is hilly. I like it. My arms are cut and well defined. I get asked all the time if I'm a boxer. Everyone says I look like a boxer. I'm sure they mean former boxer. Makes no never mind. I look healthy and strong. I'm also getting tons of sun.

St John has a really small downtown. Every merchant knows every other merchant. It's the same with the bar and restaurant owners. I hang out at this one particular bar/restaurant right in the middle of everything. I make small talk with the manager. She is pregnant and about to have her first child. Her husband also manages a bar, about a half-mile across town. I ask about Starr's family bar. She has not heard of it. I ask around at other bars as well and no one can place the name or the owner's name. I quickly come to the conclusion Starr was just throwing bullshit at our talking sessions. Before I came to the island, we exchanged a few short emails. I told her I got a DUI. She told me rehab was still boring but she was almost finished. I didn't tell her I was coming here.

I stop even attempting to put my clothes in the drawers. I have a few things hanging in the closet, but I would rather place them over a back of a chair or sofa. I also lay them out on the floor and bed. I do this for two reasons. One, I want to see what pieces go together. If everything is in my line of vision, then I can just grab it and build an outfit. Match the colors, textures, and styles. Two, I like being surrounded by my ideas. I like seeing the potential in every garment. Said another way, if I look at something one day and don't get inspired, the next day's casual glance at the same garment can inspire me into hours of activity. Same garment. Different day. It happens all the time. I don't want to miss out on an idea because I forgot something at the bottom of a drawer. Don't get me started on accessories. I've also started cutting brand new clothes with scissors to layer some pieces. Even more fun is to tear the new clothes and make them work with my ideas. This can add character the designer or manufacturer never intended. It works for me. Sometimes it works quite well.

I have purchased a school notebook and a box of colored pencils from the local grocery store. The same place I get my vodka. This is the beginning of my drawing and writing phase. I start playing with the alphabet. I'm particularly fascinated with the capital letter B. It looks like a 1 and a 3 placed next to each other. B is the second letter. Three minus one is two. Two is the second number. Hmmm.

One of my first drawings is a scene from The Fly, the Jeff Goldblum film where he accidentally turns into a human fly. I've drawn the scene in the coffee shop where he salivates onto his doughnut so it can dissolve and be easily digested. I also have him drinking coffee out of his clawed hand (that's not in the movie). It's a pretty amateur drawing. If you saw it you would understand it's meaning though. Which is: These aliens are turning me into some kind of half man, half insect alien. It's starting with my feet. A small bump is forming on the outside of each foot. When the skin breaks, they will be miniature claws. Not sure what purpose they will serve. I've been happy with my feet my entire life. They've given me few problems, but what can I do? This alien species is so advanced, they can genetically modify humans with the ease we genetically modify plants.

Chapter 8

May 2012

    I'm on an exploration of symbols, playing with mostly letters and sometimes words. I spend hours deconstructing each letter and its position in the alphabet. Very childish and very informative. I will spend hours writing in these notebooks. It helps pass the time when I feel the crushing loneliness of being so far from home. And I am far from home. I have no idea how many light years because the insect aliens won't tell me. They are just watching me. Experimenting. I'm trapped on this Island. They are running tests on me all the time. This isn't even St John. It's an impressive replica they built on their spaceship so I don't totally freak out about my captivity. They are learning everything about us humans. Through me. They are here to help, but it doesn't feel that way to me.

    I have built a structure in my room above my bed. Using the fan as a fulcrum, dozens of strings hang down from the center and stretch across the room. I attach the strings to various pieces of furniture on the floor and throughout the room. I use both reading lights on each side of the bed. I use the corners of the mirror above the dresser facing the bed. It looks like a spider web, but it's not. It's a map of their galaxy. I hang different pieces of jewelry at various places along the strings. These are the planets. I add different items each day. Move things around from time to time. It becomes more and more complex. When I lie in the bed, I look up at the fan and the surrounding strings. It's like I'm a fly caught in the middle of a giant spider web. In reality, I'm a human captive on an alien ship moving farther and farther from Earth.

I tell the hotel management to make sure they tell the cleaning lady not to pick up my clothes or move anything in my room. I just want her to empty the trash, clean the bathroom, and wipe down the kitchen area. After a few days she stops coming in the room all together. I know she is talking about me to the rest of the staff. When I'm gone they look in the room and wonder what the hell I'm doing. After a week, they all stay clear of me.

I'm really wasted. It's a mixture of vodka, coke, and weed. The aliens want to show me how to travel through time. They telepathically communicate with me all the time now. I'm getting used to having them in my brain. I can feel a slight shift when they are inside my head. Interestingly, they don't speak. They can somehow artificially fire the synaptic nerves associated with the words stored in my brain/memory. They fire off the right sequence of words, and next thing you know I've got a sentence, a thought, an idea. It's cool as long as I know they're doing it. It's how they choose to communicate.

For time travel, I need to get the room ready. I write the numbers 3, 6, 9, and 12 on big sheets of notebook paper in all different colors. I lay them out like a clock face in the middle of the room, far enough apart so my body fits in between the numbers. I need an empty beer bottle. I also need to be naked. They instruct me to lie on my back in the middle of the living room area. I have to move a lot of stuff out of the way to make room. I'm told to place the top of the beer bottle right up against my asshole. I then take my right leg and curl it up so the heel of my right foot is placed against the bottom of the bottle. I take both arms and put them on each side of my head like I'm going to do a sit-up. All set. At the same time I curl my head down, I force the bottle up my ass with my right heel. I slide down so the bottle can work its way up my asshole. I also use the leverage of my right foot. I'm doing the best I can to shove this bottle as far up my ass as possible. It hurts like hell. But I really want to time travel, so I keep it up. My eyes are shut, so as far as I know it's working. With one last push of my heel, I let out a scream and open my eyes.

It doesn't work. I'm still here in the same room. I keep my eyes fixed on the ceiling. I'm uncomfortable. I straighten my right leg and this relieves some of the pressure from my asshole. The only change I'm aware of is now I have a beer bottle up my ass. I don't know how far, but I have to get it out. I reach down with my right hand and grab hold of the bottle. I give it a hard pull thinking my intestines may come out with the suction. It comes out easily. In fact, I didn't even get it past the screwy glass part at the top. I have a really tight asshole. No blood. Nothing. Other than a little shit on the top of the bottle, you wouldn't even know it happened. I wrap the bottle in a paper towel and throw it away. I wash my hands too.

I've learned a few things from this experience. First, humans can be made to do pretty much anything. Second, the aliens have a sense of humor.

It's a few days later and I'm wasted again. I'm also horny. I can't remember the last time I had sex. I've been gone for months, and Christie and I were arguing before that, so it's been awhile. I can't stream any porn because my phone has no service on the island. How am I going to jerk off with no porn? It's possible, but it just takes longer to get going. I need some kind of catalyst. I know just the thing. I have the Christina Aguilera video for "Not Myself Tonight." While this is a far cry from porn, it certainly shows enough side boob to get me started. I need a visual to get going, then I can finish with some fantasy.

Five minutes later I start to cum. It's a fuck-ton of jizz. It's some kind of a mother load. It's spewing everywhere. Porn worthy. Then this: At the same time my seed is shooting through the air, three Giant Invisible Intergalactic Cum-Eating Ants appear and start gobbling it down. While it's still in mid flight! They don't even wait for it to land on my stomach. It's like the scene in The Karate Kid when Mr Miagi catches a fly with his chopsticks. These motherfucking aliens are harvesting my cum. Not cool! The aliens had their fun with the time travel, but this? This has to violate some intergalactic space treaty. This has to be illegal in all galaxies, not just the Milky Way.

They explain to me that the Giant Invisible Intergalactic Cum-Eating Ants are not the same aliens who are using me for experiments. My captors are educating me on the infinite biodiversity throughout the universe. Humans think we are at the top of the food chain. We aren't even close. These ants have been snatching up teenage boy cum for millennia and we aren't even aware of it. A species of ants more advanced than humans. Humbling. The aliens studying me are even more advanced. I will learn about them as the months progress. The ants have no interest in us other than our cum. It's a main source of food on their home planet: human cum. Ew.

When I am not in my room, I'm walking through the town and over the mountain passes to the private beaches. Music is usually in my ears. But sometimes, out here, I listen to the ocean. "The Ocean Loves Me" is a new refrain that I will say over and over again in the coming months. Even the coming years. I love this place in spite of the alien abuse. The people are warm and friendly. By the second week here many locals know me. Every few days I have to go to the manager and extend my stay. He usually says no problem. But this Friday they have booked the room. My room! I must be out by 6 that night. I ignore him. I literally thought he would just forget or get another room. This is my place. Look at all the work I've put into it! I assume he will just find them another room.

But at 8 he is banging on my door. "Look, Mr. Matte, you have to get out! I've got people coming in soon and the room needs to be clean." You're serious? "YES! I'm serious. Why wouldn't I be serious?" I don't know really. Everyone is so laid back on the island. Now, I'm getting pissed. You should have given me more time to pack. "Mr. Matte, I told you every day for the last few days." I must be forgetting things. Give me a second and I will start packing. He looks at the structure and all my mess. He doesn't say anything. Then he offers to help too. They really want me out of here. He also offers his car as transportation to the next hotel, conveniently located about a quarter-mile away. It takes about an hour to pull everything down and pack his car. He tries to be nice on the sixty-second trip. By the time we get there, he is calm and apologizes for losing it. No worries, I tell him. He won't forget me any time soon.

I check in to the new hotel where I will stay for the next five nights. It's much more luxurious than the other place. I wish I'd found it first. More importantly, the phones work. I can finally get in touch with Christie and the kids. I get through to Christie and she tells me she thought I was dead. It has been over a month since we talked. I start crying and telling her how much I miss her and the kids. I'm so lonely. The night before I was kicked out of the hotel, I was wailing at the top of my lungs from some existential grief. The song "Halo" by Beyoncé was on a continuous repeat. I'm not sure how long I moaned. Hours I think. Talking to Christie makes me feel a little better. She tells me the divorce is going to be final in a few weeks. I never showed up at the hearing. She gets everything. I'm happy for her. I'm not mad anymore. Just sad. She can sense my hurt and stays on the phone with me. She is kinder than she has any right to be. She is a loyal and wonderful person. This is why I fell in love with her.

We never speak of her business empire. I just want to talk about the kids. This is starting to have an effect on their schoolwork. Especially my oldest. School will be out in a few weeks. They need the break. I ask to speak with Austin, but he doesn't want to come to the phone. Christie puts my youngest on the line, but it's not him. I can tell it's some kind of alien imposter. We speak for only a short time. He tells me he loves me. This is too much. I hang up with Christie and cry for hours.

I try to think of some kind of plan. To do what? I don't know. I can't stay on the island forever. I talk to Christie every day while I'm at this hotel. I never really unpack. I've spent a total of three weeks on St John. For some reason, I decide to head over to St. Thomas and check it out. It's much bigger than St. John.

Chapter 9

May 2012

    I check in to the St. Thomas Ritz-Carlton. While I'm registering, I notice a large, hand-drawn map of the islands behind the counter. There's a boat pictured with the words "S.S Minnow" on the side – the shipwrecked boat from the TV show Gilligan's Island. I watched it all the time as a kid. I'm in a good mood and want to talk to someone. I ask the clerk if she watched Gilligan's Island growing up too. She is younger than me, but with syndication you never know. She answers quickly. "No, but I read the book. We had to read it in high school." She's not trying to be funny. She's obviously thinking of Robinson Crusoe or Gulliver's Travels. It strikes me as funny and I start having a laughing fit, right there in the lobby of the Ritz-Carlton, St Thomas. The people behind me see that I'm alone and trying to hold in what can best be described as the church giggles. This goes on for the next few minutes until she is finished checking me in. It's the first time I truly laughed at something in months. It felt good.

    I grab lunch, and the waitress takes a shine to me. She's my age, maybe older. But of course it's not her. It's not an alien either. It's Steve Martin. The comedian. Not sure how he managed to get inside this black middle-age waitress, but I really don't care. He has me in stitches for the next two hours. My sides are aching by the time I walk to my room.

My taxi driver on St Thomas is named "Big Love." He's a young guy, maybe twenty-five years old. Someone has spray-painted his name on different rocks and near landmarks throughout the main roads of the island. It's guerrilla marketing at its best. People even shout his name when we drive by. He just happened to be near the ferry when I came back. We hit it off. He is cool but straight edge. No drugs will be coming from this guy. He thinks I could get some in the outdoor market, but he really doesn't know. By the time I leave for London a week later, he will be helping me pack some of my clothes in boxes for DHR Transport. I need to ship some stuff by airmail. I've accumulated too much luggage, even for flying first-class to England. I send them to the Dorchester Hotel, where I plan on staying. I don't have a reservation of course; I just assume they'll have a room for me. Clearly, I'm still having problems with the executive planning area in my brain. I've recently been listening to No Doubt and Gwen Stefani's solo albums. Gwen Stefani will be my muse for the next few months. No Doubt. She doesn't even live in London, but I need to go there first. I will get instructions when I arrive.

Before London, I have some final island time. I spend almost all of it in my room. I have my clothes laid out in a circle so I can find exactly what I want when I want it. I move the furniture around too. I'm glad I don't have to recreate the structure from my last room. I spend most every day getting high and writing in my notebooks. The aliens are expecting more from me now. They are using me as a human Enigma machine. The Enigma machine was a

Nazi coding device used to send secret military messages during World War II. It was very hard for the Allies to break. When they finally did, with the help of Alan Turing, it was a turning point in the war. This time the good aliens have an advanced, not yet fully functioning Biological Enigma Machine: me. The bad aliens, different species, can't seem to find a workable human Enigma Machine. There are many of us. But with the Earth population of around eight billion people, it takes time. Even for them. Hell, the bad aliens are so lost at this point they aren't even sure if humans are capable of achieving this kind of communication. They are becoming more and more convinced that human telepathy will never evolve. They can make some humans act through telepathy, but it's only one way. They have been unsuccessful in their ability to make the humans aware they are being influenced. They want some of us to communicate with them. They need our assistance and our planet.

    I'm trying to make this as simple as possible. Good and bad aliens – that's all I'm getting from my captors/guardians at this point. I will learn more and my vocabulary will evolve as my telepathic skills develop. Much later, I'll see what my captors/guardians look like (not insect-like). I will also see and communicate with the bad aliens, some of them anyway (also not insect-like). We don't get a lot of respect from these guys, but that's going to bite them in the ass before long. Let's just say they are on the wrong side of history with regards to telepathy and the evolution of humans.

    I notice that phrases start to pop into my head fully formed: "Orange is Indigo," "Only 4 get thru," "U-Turn at 21." There are others, but these are the sticky ones – along with "I'm Job, I love you Eve" and "The Ocean Loves Me." Five different phrases and I have to figure out what they mean. It's an important job and I'm up for the task. I will spend hundreds of hours over the next few years figuring this shit out. I want to do my part for the preventive-alien war effort. They have not told me why there might be a war. When this is resolved, humans will be rewarded with a completely new understanding of the brain. New technologies and new advances in biology and genetics. Every science will be advanced because of our assistance with keeping peace in this part of the galaxy. I'm not the only human helping either. There are many more. They just won't tell me who. The reason is simple: The bad aliens can scan our brains and read our every thought. They can read fear and love and every other human emotion. They know when we're lying. They can also tell if we believe something is true by scanning our minds. This is one of their most powerful tools, if not the most powerful tool they have. Scanning certain types of biological minds. Both, individually and collectively. Once they know a human mind completely, that human mind can be made to do their bidding. The human isn't even aware of it. The unknowing human thinks their thoughts are their own. However, some human minds are unreadable. Some others will simply not do the malevolent alien bidding. Some of us are not built for violence. Anger? Yes. Violence? This is a primitive response that will stop serving us in the future. This is very important for humanity's survival, our evolution. It's also a thorn in the side of the aliens.

One of our greatest defense mechanisms against total alien domination is for humans to be able to look at the exact same information and come up with diametrically opposed conclusions. For example: Darwin's theory of evolution. A million different minds have a million different opinions. Some subtly different, some in direct conflict with the other. This infuriates them. They only understand total obedience to one worldview. When they scan our collective minds, they actually become confused. This makes them weaker. They don't know what action to take. They don't know what actions we will take! As a collective conscience, humans can kick some alien ass. Or at least keep them at bay.

I'm going through the St Thomas airport when I get pulled aside for an extra security check. I'm sent into a side room where two TSA guys spend about forty-five minutes going through my luggage. They see all my notebooks and writing. They ask me if I'm carrying any drugs. No, I would never travel with illegal drugs. Ever. They look at me with an extra amount of suspicion. I assume it's because I'm dressed a bit unusual. They finally let me pass. My flight to London is first class with a layover in Miami. By the time we land in Miami, I'm too claustrophobic to finish the flight to London. I haven't been near this many people in a long time. My headphones are in my ears constantly. I don't want to talk to anyone. My luggage flies ahead but I leave the airport and head toward Miami Beach. I still need the beach. I figure I will spend the night and continue on the next day. I end up staying a few days; it prepares me to start interacting with people again. I've spent a lot of time alone. I need to get used to people. I buy some new clothes on Lincoln Avenue and some coke too. Coke is easy to get in Miami.

My luggage is waiting for me when I finally arrive in London. I call Christie. My phone works here with a few tweaks. She tells me our divorce is final. This makes me terribly sad. We spent our honeymoon in London thirteen years earlier. I know she is sad too. We don't know what else to say to each other. We hang up. I try to check in to the Dorchester Hotel. There are no rooms available; I end up checking into a Westin a few blocks away. I need to find some drugs fast to numb the pain. I take the tube to Camden, one of the coolest places in all of London. It's part flea market, part global trading post. You can find anything here. I find a dealer within an hour. He supplies me for my entire stay in London. Camden is way too hip for me, but I don't care. I love the people and the shops. I will end up spending two to three hours a day here, practically every day.

It's in London when the idea finally crystallizes that I will become a stylist for celebrities, starting with Gwen Stefani, my muse. It's really the first time I have a cogent plan to do something since I started traveling/losing my mind. I also start using the term remixing to describe what I can do with clothes and fashion. I still see colors in a way I never have before. I'm not a designer. I know nothing about the manufacturing of clothes. I'm a pseudo stylist with some avant-garde ideas. Some great, some not so great. I like the word *remixer* though. It has a musical element to it. It feels right.

The time I stay in London is both focused and productive. It's also painful. I can't help but think back on the time we came for a spring-break family vacation just two short years ago. It seems like a lifetime. It was one of our favorite family trips. We rented a condominium just a few blocks from Harrods department store. One night Austin, Christie, and I went to one of Gordon Ramsey's new restaurants. It had just opened and was receiving rave reviews. Austin ordered a chocolate dessert sphere that melted before your eyes when the waiter added another layer of hotter chocolate on top. Another memory is of Carson and me walking through Green Park and the squirrels running up and down his legs trying to snatch peanuts out of his hands. When we told Austin and Christie later that evening, they didn't believe us. So we had to go back the next day and video it using my iPhone. That evening we all laughed in amazement at the bravery of the squirrels and at Carson's ability to hold perfectly still while they ran up and down the sides of his legs. My favorite memory was when Austin, Carson, and I walked into the condo to find a perfectly prepared home-cooked Easter dinner. While all the boys were out sightseeing, Christie had stayed behind, gone shopping at the corner grocery, and surprised us with what can only be described as the perfect Easter feast. We were a happy family. Once. I try not to think about these things now. It hurts too much.

In spite of the pain, I have no thoughts of being followed by satellites, possessed by demons, or communicating with aliens. No imposter people either. It's a time for creating. I have more ideas here than I've had before. Fueled by the city and my music, I'm unstoppable. I start going to bars and talking to people again. If not talking, then I'm observing. I almost always get positive comments on my styles. Occasionally I go a bit overboard and create something that is more costume than fashion. But, hey, live and learn.

Chapter 10

May 2012

After about a week, I check in to 45 Park Lane Hotel, across the street from the Dorchester, both owned by the same company, which is owned by the Sultan of Brunei. It's new, maybe a year old. The place is plush, and it's located in one of the wealthiest parts of London. My room number is 45. Easy to remember: 45 at 45 Park Lane.

As soon as I arrive, I completely redecorate my room. I've purchased flags, scarves, even large pieces of leather from Camden. I cover the sofas and the chairs with my new purchases. I hang jewelry from the lights. It feels like home. It's like my place in St John but not as crazy. More stylish.

Every floor has a personal valet. It's early evening and I get a knock on the door. It's my personal Jeeves, only he's French. He comes in the room and can't hide the delight in his eyes. "Monsieur! What is this? I have never seen anybody do this before. This is fantastic. How long did it take you? I love the colors. How fun is this? Do you mind if I show my co-workers? Are you some kind of artist? Would I have seen your work in a museum?" Needless to say, we hit it off. I didn't even care if he was faking it. He works for tips and his response may have been a bit of a show. I don't think so, though, because it's hard to fake smiling eyes. It felt good for him to acknowledge the work, the talent.

I go down to the hotel bar to grab a burger. As I walk in, I see a portrait of Gwen Stefani above the lounge area. I can't believe my eyes! This is obviously a sign from the universe. After my meal, I ask my French Jeeves if he can get someone to put the portrait in my room. Change it out with another photo. The next day he tells me it's not possible; it's bolted to the wall. It really doesn't bother me that much. But it's still a sign, a beautiful sign. Thanks, Universe.

I put my drawings and writings aside for the time I'm in London. I'm really focused on the fashion side of things. I have my French Jeeves call Gwen Stefani's business manager and set up a meeting for when I arrive in Los Angeles the following week. I also ask him to make reservations at the Beverly Hills Hotel, the same place I was run out of by demons just over a month ago. None of this is on my mind. I'm focused on what I will show Gwen and her manager at that first meeting. This London trip puts yet another interesting spin on my psychosis. It would be easy to say that I'm delusional thinking I'll work for Gwen Stefani. You would have a harder time convincing someone I was psychotic. I may be eccentric, but I'm not dangerous anymore.

One of the last things I buy before I leave London is a white Burberry Raincoat for Ms. Stefani. I also buy some gloves and a scarf. My final purchase is a pair of Chrome Hearts sunglasses. I spend about $2,500. A risky investment? I don't think so. I know Gwen Stefani will love it. All of it.

On the flight back to the States, I create a new game on the plane. It's sort of a combination of word jumbles and words with friends. Even a bit of Sudoku. This creation is directly related to one of the symptoms of schizophrenia: word salad.

I call the game Eugenius – a combination of my middle name Eugene and the word genius. I've done about ten of these. They are very difficult to create. I keep them in a special notebook that I will lose by the end of this year. I haven't taken the time to make new ones. It would be the perfect game for Twitter. Eugenius can be news- or headline-related and would get people to stay on Twitter longer while trying to create the answers. Kind of like *The New York Times* uses the crossword puzzles to keep people buried in the newspaper longer.

I arrive in LA on May 25. While going through customs, I'm again pulled aside by the TSA for additional search. The airport is packed. The Beverly Hills Hotel has a driver waiting for me outside the gates. I'm told to wait in a room filled with people from what seems like every country on Earth. I take a seat and wait thirty minutes. Nothing. I'm getting impatient and a little worried. What did I do now? I go up to one of the many security guards and tell him I have a driver waiting. How long is this going to take? He asks for my passport and walks me over to a counter with a computer. I can't see the computer screen. He pulls up some info and asks if I'm carrying any illegal drugs.

"No, sir."

"Do you mind if I search your backpack?"

I don't answer, just hand it to him. He doesn't open it. He asks me again if I have any illegal drugs. I assure him I do not.

"OK, you can leave."

"That's it? Thank you." I find the driver, get my luggage, and head toward the hotel.

This is the second time I've been pulled aside for additional search by the TSA. I'm starting to wonder what's going on. It will be another few months before I'm even aware of the bench warrant for my arrest. I never showed up at pre-trial. I signed an agreement to this when I bailed out of jail. I don't remember. When I hired the lawyer, I was expecting him to take care of everything and keep me posted on a trial date. My lawyer neglected to remind me. He doesn't even know there is a bench warrant. He never said a word about pre-trial in the few conversations I've had with him. The law doesn't care how competent your lawyer is. I learn this the hard way. I'm not yet versed in the criminal justice system. All my legal experience has been with lawyers at the transactional level. This is a whole new world, and I am not a fan.

The valet guy at the Beverly Hills Hotel walks me to my room. It's beautiful, even nicer than the last time. They were making significant renovations throughout the hotel last time I was here. Now most of the work is done. The hotel never called me about my clothes. They sent me a checkout email, but I never got a call about my belongings. I'm curious to see what they did with them. I give the valet a few hundred dollars and ask him to talk to the manager and see if they can locate my clothes. I explain how the last time I was here I was called out on business and had to leave in a hurry. About an hour later I get a knock on my door. It's the valet guy with an assistant. They have all my clothes! Jewelry. Everything. They even pulled a $1,000 bottle of cologne out of the toilet. I tried to flush it during the night of the demons. I'm really impressed with the cleaning people. I guess this kind of thing happens more than I know. In any case, I have tons of clothes. Piles of them. I can't fit everything in the drawers. The closet is stuffed with jackets, sweaters, shirts, etc. I lay additional pieces everywhere. The living area. Across the bed. The bathroom floor. I love the mess. Well, it's not a mess, it's a work of art in progress.

I have no thoughts of demons, either. Clearly I was mistaken about them. Again. A few things in my brain misfired and some signals got crossed. There are no more demons and no more satellites following me. I will continue to have delusions about Christie, imposter people, and aliens, but the paranoia is receding. I can't even access that feeling anymore. That's not entirely true, but that's how it feels now. Even when I'm on coke, it's just not there. This is another shift my brain is making while I'm not paying attention.

The paranoia will come back for a final showdown later in the year, but I don't know it yet. When it does come back, it fights with everything it has. It wants to stay alive. It rips my mind apart with fear. But I beat it. Somehow, I beat that fucker to death.

I send Starr a short email and tell her I spent some time in St John. I tell her it would be nice to hear from her. She doesn't respond. That's another thing about rehab. Everyone says they're going to stay in touch, but they don't.

It's around 3 in the morning. My first night back in the States, and I'm having trouble sleeping because of the time change from England. I take a shower and get dressed. A new light gray Armani suede jacket, with a new charcoal Armani gray scarf. A new pair of slightly faded jeans with a pair of midnight blue suede shoes. Headphones in, listening to Jay-Z, "Empire State of Mind." I feel good. I look good. I have no idea why I take the time to get so overdressed. I'm glad I did, though. I have so many clothes, I might as well wear them. The cab drops me off in front of Mel's Drive-In on Sunset. It's open twenty-four hours. I immediately notice a pretty brunette standing outside at the entrance, smoking a cigarette. She looks to be in her late twenties. I have to walk by her to get inside. Most people ignore you when you have headphones in. They take it as a hint that you're not interested in talking. She is staring at me as I'm walking toward her. I make eye contact and smile. I can't help myself. She's grinning at me from ear to ear. "Look at you! I bet you just came from Europe. American men would never wear a scarf that way."

I pull out my earphones. "Excuse me?"

She says it again. She has a slight Russian accent.

She introduces herself as Alena and tells me to come sit inside with her and her friend. I'm immediately on guard, but I follow her to the table. She is going to play me somehow, pick my pocket or some such nonsense. No one is this nice in LA. No one is this nice anywhere. She starts peppering me with questions. I tell her I just flew in from London and I'm staying at the Beverly Hills Hotel. "Expensive place," she says. She wants to know why I look so nice at 3 a.m. I explain how I'm going to meet with Gwen Stefani's business manager in a few days and get into remixing clothes for celebrities. I need to dress the part. I tell her of my recent divorce and island travels. I warm up to her in spite of my initial defenses. The thought in the back of my mind is that she might be a prostitute. She's not. She tells me she's also divorced. Her ex lives in Russia. She came to LA to start over. She works at an apartment rental agency.

I order a burger and a shake. Her friend becomes invisible. We talk for another hour. Her friend finally wants to leave, and since she's driving, she has to go too. She gets up to leave and asks for my phone. I hand it to her without thinking. She dials her number with my cell. I hear her phone ring. She answers it and immediately puts me in as a contact. She creates a contact on my phone for her: "Alena." She hands me back my phone and tells me she will text me tomorrow. We will go out. It will be fun. She turns and walks out of the restaurant.

Chapter 11

May 2012

 I finally get to sleep around 7 a.m. I put a do-not-disturb sign on the door. Around 2 in the afternoon, I roll out of bed. I think back on the night before and wonder if I will hear from Alena. I pick up my phone. I already have two texts. One from 12:30: "You awake?" Another from 1:45: "Text me when you get up. Let's grab something to eat." These messages please me a great deal. I have someone who wants to hang out. The fact that she is a pretty Russian woman intrigues me as well. I will soon learn there are plenty of pretty Russian women in LA. I'm still not sure of her motives, but what have I got to lose.

 We meet for a late lunch in the Polo Lounge of the Beverly Hills Hotel. She looks even better than the night before. She turns heads when she walks in the room. With her heels on, she is about four inches taller than me. This turns me on. We continue our conversation from the night before. She is kinda-dating some guy who wants to break into the music business. He is supposedly a really talented rapper. I'm glad she tells me she has a boyfriend. It puts me right in the friend zone. Exactly where I want to be. I tell her about my family, my ex-wife and how much I miss my kids. My former life as an advertising executive. We share a bunch of stories. It's nice. By the end of lunch, she is telling me I should come with her to a new club opening the following night. We will be on the VIP list. I might meet some people with connections to the fashion and movie industry. Sounds like a great idea. I tell her that I have a driver who will pick her up. What time? She will meet me here at the hotel at 10. It will be easier if we just leave from here. Fine. That works for me.

We arrive at the nightclub around 11. There is a long line wrapped around the side of the building. Sonny drops us off right at the front, next to the bouncers and the velvet ropes. Alena gives them our name and we get whisked right in. Good thing too. There is no way I want to wait in line at a club. I hated it when I was twenty-five and I cringe at the idea of doing it again. Inside we meet the promoter of the club who pays us special attention. We have a private area set aside. I order a bottle of vodka, not worrying about the cost. The place is packed and loud. It doesn't matter to me, though. As usual, I have my headphones in. Even when I turn them all the way up, the sound still gets past the ear buds. The vibrations also move up my legs and through my body. The music is club music. No lyrics. Why would I listen to music without lyrics? I wouldn't know what to do or think. I need words. I need music too, as it touches a different part of my soul. But at this point, the lyrics help guide and instruct me.

I go to the bathroom and do some coke. Such a cliché. There are two stalls. One is occupied. I can hear the guy inside snorting away. I didn't think Millennial's did coke. I thought it was an old school drug. Apparently not. I go in the other stall and try to be a bit more discreet. The valet turns the water on for me to wash my hands. I wash them quickly and throw a $20 bill in his basket. He gives me a big grin. "Thank you, sir." He doesn't give a fuck about the drugs. All told, I make five trips to the bathroom. Alena and I shut the place down. It costs me $100 to pee that night.

On the ride back to the hotel, Alena tells me to take out my headphones. I'm being rude and she wants to talk. She actually says that: I'm being rude. We didn't talk that much at the club. She went off to hang with some friends and I sat there mostly ignoring people. Occasionally talking to the club promoter, or the waitress.

We get back to the hotel around 3:30 a.m. Alena wants to come see the room. I want her company. I also want her to see my design ideas. In the room, I make us a few drinks. She knows I've been doing coke but doesn't want any. At least not tonight. In the hotel room, I have less of a problem taking out my headphones. I drop in one of the few CDs I purchased in London and we listen to music through the stereo.

She looks around at the mess I've left everywhere and doesn't seem to mind in the least. No judgments, no comments on what a slob I am, just curiosity. She picks up a few pieces and nods her head in approval. We smile at each other. She notices one of my notebooks on the desk and asks if she can look inside. Sure. She skims a few pages and stops on a lilac tree I started drawing earlier in the day. My colored pencils are lying next to the notebook. She picks one up and says, "May I?" Before I can reply, she picks up the notebook and pencils and places them on the carpet. "We can finish it together." She starts to color in one of the branches, using the correct shade of brown. By correct. I mean that I would have used the same color. It's just a bit softer than the brown I used as an outline for the tree. I lay down across from her and pick up a pencil to start working on the flowers. We talk about her childhood in Russia and how one of her favorite things was to color. We talk about her mother. She misses her mother. We talk about a lot of things. There is a sweetness about her that is undeniable. She has cast a spell on me. I've known her for twenty-four hours and she has stolen a piece of my heart.

She is tired and wants to go to sleep. Can she sleep here tonight? Sure, take the bed. I'm not tired anyway. I'm going to stay up and work on some other drawings. I refuse to consider she is making a pass at me. She's tired, like she says.

"Do you have a T-shirt I can sleep in"?

What? Yes. No! Stop talking. I don't say that of course. I tell her to pick anything that she thinks looks comfortable. I grab the notebook and pencils and head to the bathroom. The bathrooms at the Beverly Hills Hotel are large. I can draw on the floor in there.

I'm rocking back in forth on the floor. Beyoncé's "Halo" repeats in my ears. I'm leaning over my notebook, crying. I don't know why. I hurt because I miss Christie. I hurt because I miss my kids. I hurt because Alena misses her mother. I'm completely oblivious to the sobbing sounds I'm making. I hear a noise and look up. Alena has stuck her head around the corner of the bathroom. How long has she been there? I pull out my earphones. She says, "Come lay down. You're hurting and you need to get some rest."

I wipe my eyes clean. I'm tired too, in spite of the coke. "OK, I'll be right there." She shuts the door.

Why didn't she say, "Are you OK?" That's what most people would say. Why didn't she say, "What's wrong?" That's what other people would say. She somehow knew what I was thinking and feeling. And she still likes me. Strange. I lie down on top of the bed and pass out. I wake up a few hours later to a handwritten note: "Let's go to

Venice Beach this afternoon. Text me when you get up. You snore loud! Me."

I almost forgot. Today is the day I'm supposed to meet with Gwen Stefani's manager. Sonny picks me up around 12:30 and we head over to my 1 p.m. appointment. His office is right in the heart of the Beverly Hills shopping district, next to Saks Fifth Avenue. Sonny drops me off at the entrance. I tell him to wait, I don't know how long I'm going to be. There are two women at the reception area. I give them the name provided to me by French Jeeves. "Sorry, sir, there is no one here by that name." I'm shocked. French Jeeves was nothing if not thorough. The other woman jumps in. "I think he used to have an office here but he moved out recently." This is an unforeseen setback. I wonder if he thinks I'm a no show at his new address. There's nothing I can do about it now. But I'm not going to let it ruin my day. I get back in the car and tell Sonny what's going on.

"Where to now?"

"Let's go back to the hotel so I can get changed. I'm going to Venice Beach with Alena."

"Sounds like a plan," he says. Sonny will spend a good bit of time waiting in his limo for Alena and me. I text Alena and tell her we will be going to the beach earlier than expected. "When can you be ready? See you at the hotel in about an hour. I'm looking forward to the beach."

Sonny drops us off in Santa Monica in front of the pier. My spirits are high. So am I. I also have a companion for the first time in six months – someone to talk to and hang out with. It feels good. It feels great. We hang out on the pier for a bit and then start toward Venice Beach. It's about three miles south of the Santa Monica pier. An hour's walk. I tell Sonny to drive that way and I'll call him when we are ready. The weed shops in Venice Beach are as numerous as the restaurants. Not interested. I buy a pair of Hello Kitty boots at one of the shoe stores. I'm not sure what I will do with them, but I like the color. I buy a few other items for later use. Tourists are everywhere. Homeless people are everywhere. Today I'm one of the tourists.

Chapter 12

May 2012

On the way back to the hotel, we swing by Alena's current boyfriend's apartment, if you can call it that. It's really just a ten-by-ten-foot room. There's no bed, just a mattress in the middle of the floor. He has a desk and a fridge, but no kitchen area. There's a small bathroom with a shower and a toilet. I didn't know they rented places like this. Ken is younger than Alena. He looks barely old enough to drink. He has a big tattoo on his neck; it must have hurt like hell. Someone told him he raps faster than Eminem. As fast as Busta Rhymes. I listen to a few of his songs. They don't suck. He needs a producer. Why did we come here? He can get us some good coke.

I've started videoing myself with my iPhone. The reason is this: I've started noticing more instances of synchronicity. Meaningful coincidences. The incident in New York with the J.Lo video is starting to happen everyday now. I want to get them on video for people to see. I remember studying Carl Jung (the father of synchronicity) in college and being intrigued by this concept. I have numerous instances of synchronistic events daily. I would be a fool to ignore them. Even if we forget the concept of meaningful coincidence for a moment, these moments are meaningful. I'm noticing things that most people miss.

A common example teachers use to explain synchronicity is this: You think of a friend you haven't thought about in five years and the phone rings. It's your friend. You can't believe it. What are the odds? This or something like this has happened to most people at least once in their lives. It happens to me every day. Multiple times a day.

Let me give you another example. We are driving down Cloverfield Boulevard. I'm in the back of the limo daydreaming, wondering if my son is taking his piano lesson. Sonny gets my attention, asking me if I want to grab some food. Why not? He suggests pizza. Sounds good to me. A few minutes later we pull into a local pizza place. On the side of a building I see an ad. Piano lessons for kids. This is what I'm talking about. Everyday.

The problem is this: I can explain this to you and perhaps you think it's cool. If you are a cynic, you will find an infinite number of reasons to dismiss it. That doesn't work for me. I'm a skeptic, not a cynic. I've found a way to show people all the synchronistic events that happen to me. Here's how: First, I put my iPhone music on random. Second, I just start spouting stream-of-consciousness thoughts. Third, I video. Everytime, without fail, I will think something and then verbalize it for the video. Soon enough, sometimes at the exact moment, a song plays that "coincidentally" happens to reference that something I just mentioned in the previous few seconds or minutes. How is this possible? I have no idea.

A skeptic would say that once a song starts, my mind unconsciously knows what lyrics are coming next and my stream of consciousness is influenced by the music. I would say, of course! How could it be otherwise? Then I would tell them that it even works for songs that I don't know are on the playlist. It will even work for a playlist that you made and asked me to listen to. My brain somehow knows things at a deeper level than I ever imagined. Not just mine. All of ours. We just need to pay attention.

Another example: I'm walking down Lincoln Boulevard in Santa Monica. It's not really a main tourist area. It's a busy street. Lots of traffic. It's the middle of the day. I'm not sure why I turned down this street. A man pulls up next to me and asks if I can help him with directions to the airport. I'm about tell him no when he pulls into the parking lot in front of me. He stops, waiting for my directions. I lean into his open passenger side window. He has a heavy Italian accent and is dressed in an expensive suit. On my left hand, I'm wearing two-inch-long mahogany bead bracelet. It's made with small wooden beads held together by tiny elastic bands. In other words, it stretches when you pull on it. I purchased it in Camden last month. I bought a few of them in different colors. I've attached a pair of yellow Paul Smith cufflinks. They spell the word LOVE. I've stuck them through the beads the same way you would stick a cufflink through a shirt hole. The cufflinks don't lay flat like they do on a sleeve. They look like they are standing up with the silver metal part exposed. It's unique and different.

The Italian guy notices my wrist and asks to take a closer look. He asks where I bought it. I tell him I made it, it was simple really. I tell him a bit about my new career. He gives me a big knowing smile, like he is sharing a secret with me. He asks me if he can have it to show his boss? He pulls out his business card and hands it to me. He is V.P of sales for Giorgio Armani, the Italian fashion designer. He thinks he would love it. I take it off my wrist and hand it to him.

He thanks me and takes my cell number. He will call me. He drives off. I never hear from him again. Perhaps he called and I never answered. Doubtful.

I try to imagine the chances of me randomly meeting a Giorgio Armani rep on a busy industrial street in LA. I will eventually come to believe that figuring the odds of something happening through synchronicity completely misses the point. It's like figuring out the odds of seeing a double rainbow. You miss the beauty if you try to figure out the why. It's more fun to just roll with it, appreciate it.

One more example: This one goes beyond synchronicity and falls into the realm of the spiritual or mystic. It was as if a director or choreographer had staged my every step to be in sync with the music playing in my headphones. The surrounding landscape, the moving cars and trucks, even the gardener who was trimming the hedges – all their movements were somehow choreographed to be in sync with the music playing in my ears! The music that only I could hear. What I was seeing was impossible. Yet it was happening right before my eyes. It was like the J.Lo video in New York but times a hundred. Times ten thousand. Since I was used to being followed by satellites, I thought they had staged the whole scene and were somehow mocking me to see how I would react. As soon as the song was over, I had to catch my breath and sit. I was awed by this experience. There was a moment of silence in between the songs on my iPhone. In that moment, I asked for God's help. Please stop these powerful people from mocking me. Please help me figure out what's going on with me. With my brain. I can't handle this anymore. Please help.

I didn't get a reply. At least I didn't think I did. It would take me a while to understand what happened. In case you were wondering what song that was playing on my iPhone, it was *Blinded by the Light* by Bruce Springsteen.

Five years later, during the summer of 2017, I will see a movie called *Baby Driver*. There is an early sequence in the film where Baby, a getaway driver and the star of the movie, picks up coffee for the rest of the gang. Baby also keeps his headphones in all the time. He needs his music to drown out a constant tinnitus hum he's had since childhood. As he's walking back to the gang hideout with the coffee, the song *Harlem Shuffle* plays in the background. Every move is choreographed. The scene is blocked to perfection. It's a work of art in staging and timing. The first time I saw the scene, I got goose bumps that lasted the entire song. This is the most accurate dramatization I've seen of what happened to me that spring day in 2012.

I'm standing in front of the Beverly Hills Hotel waiting for Sonny to pick me up. I don't feel like waiting in the valet area, so I tell him to meet me on the street in front of the hotel. This just isn't done. Everyone at the hotel wants to make an entrance or an exit. As usual, I have my headphones on. I'm also carrying my backpack. I like the weight of it on my shoulder. It has become as much a part of me as my headphones. I also have a number of beanies that I wear. My hair has gotten much longer. It's easier to throw on a beanie than take the time to style it. Sunglasses too. I wear sunglasses all the time. Even inside. At night. I want to keep people out. Alena says people think I'm on drugs when I wear them at night. She's right about that. I usually am. I just don't care. Fine. "But, please take those goddamn headphones off so we can talk," she says. "It's rude." OK. I take them out for a while. As soon as the conversation starts to drag or she gets a text from someone, the headphones go right back in.

I need to figure out how to get in touch with Gwen Stefani's manager. Her band, No Doubt, is about to release a new album for the first time in years. They've been in the studio recording for the last couple of months. They posted a video on the their website showing them jamming and talking about the new album. They also mention the fact they are recording in a Santa Monica studio. They even show a few exterior shots of the studio. No landmarks or anything. How hard could it be to find a recording studio? I figure I'll just find the studio and go directly to the source. I can turn this into an even bigger win. While in London, I also bought some items the band could wear performing.

I decide to move to the Chateau Marmont on Sunset Boulevard. It's famous for a number of reasons, one of them being that John Belushi died there from a speedball overdose in 1982. I don't do heroin, so this can't happen to me. The Chateau Marmont is much hipper than the Beverly Hills Hotel. The rooms are a bit older. The vibe is altogether different. Cool and laid back. The bar and dining area are always crowded. They get their fair share of celebrities too. Not nearly as many as the Beverly Hills Hotel, where I would literally run into a famous person every day: actors, rock stars, rap stars, TV stars, you name it. If you are a fan of Hollywood, it can be fun.

On the ride over to the new hotel, I ask Sonny if he wants to make an extra $500. "What do I have to do?" Pack all my clothes, jewelry, cufflinks, and notebooks into my suitcases and bring everything to the Chateau Marmont. I tell him it will take a few hours. I have things lying everywhere. Across the bed. Hanging from the walls. On the floor. Especially on the floor. There is a winding footpath from the door to the bed. Upon first viewing, you might think it was a mess. If you took your time and really looked, you would see that it's more like a Jackson Pollock or a Picasso.

I explain that I also soaped up the bathroom mirror like kids do on mischief night. I added graffiti to give it something extra. I was making one of my iPhone videos and thought this might add a bit of life to the place. I was also having fun making a mess. Like an eight-year-old. *No problem Tom.*

I give Sonny a few more instructions: The Beverly Hills Hotel places beautiful fresh lilies in all the suites. Different colors depending on availability. Recently they have been yellow. As usual, the color drew me in. But I wanted to make some changes to it. Play with it. I hung some red and brown feather earrings from the petals. I pushed some post earrings through the leaves. I did this on every other leaf. The post earrings are fake diamonds, emeralds and rubies. They make the light bounce around on the walls in different patterns. I dropped a gold necklace in the middle where all the pollen collects. I loved the way it falls. Some of the gold spills outside the flower down its sides. Beautiful in its asymmetry. I tell Sonny it's quite fragile so please be careful with it. *No problem Tom.*

I've also started redesigning a rose. Someone gave it to Alena the night before. The first thing I do is wrap the stem in a sky blue scarf. Now the sky is under the rose. Cool. I like the way it looks but it needs something else. I'm not sure what. I will work on it later. This is less fragile than the lily but it needs special attention as well. *No problem Tom.*

I'm at the bar in the Chateau Marmont having a drink. The bar/restaurant area is in the center of the hotel. It's lunchtime and crowded as usual. I look over and see Robin

Thicke at a big table with a bunch of other people. Robin Thicke is an R&B singer from Los Angeles. In a little over a year, he will have a huge hit with *Blurred Lines*. Today he is working on a TV show called *Duets*. I actually have a few of his songs on my iPhone. He dresses stylishly. He's taller and younger than me. It's obvious he pays attention to his clothes. Like I do. I make a note of this and store it in the back of my mind.

Chapter 13

May-June 2012

    I invite Alena over to check out my new hotel room. She loves it, especially the balcony looking up at the Hollywood Hills. Sonny was by earlier in the day and placed all my suitcases in the middle of the living area. I have seven suitcases now, packed mostly with clothes. I don't unpack everything. I can't. I don't have room. I put a few things in the closet and a few things on the bed, floor, chairs, etc. He was careful with the flowers.

    Sonny drives us to another nightclub where I might meet some connections for my new remix clothes design business. I don't of course. But we do have a good time. We will do this a few more times over the next week or so. The last time I go to a nightclub with Alena I will wear the white Burberry raincoat that I bought for Gwen Stefani. It works with a new pair of jeans. I plan on getting it dry-cleaned before our eventual meeting.

    The next day we have lunch at the hotel. Robin Thicke is here again. I mention this to Alena and she says I should go introduce myself. I tell her I'll think about it. This is the second time I've seen him in two days. I'm sure he'll be back.

I'm dressed to meet Alena for dinner. I'm wearing a light gray suede Armani jacket paired with a smoky gray Armani scarf. I'm wearing the scarf European style. We have reservations for an early meal at the Beverly Hills Hotel. On my way out of the Chateau Marmont, I step into the lobby bathroom to make sure I look good. Vanity.

Robin Thicke is washing his hands in the sink getting ready to walk out the door. He looks at me and comments, "Great look. Love the jacket." I'm not about to lose this chance. I introduce myself and shake his hand. I tell him how I remix styles as my new profession. I can do this for him, not that he needs it. He gives me a number to his assistant so we can set up a meeting. He walks out the door. I'm in a bit of shock. I look at myself in the bathroom mirror and think, You fly motherfucker, you just got your first meeting with a potential client. I can't help but notice that Robin Thicke is right: I do look great! I leave the bathroom very pleased with myself. Giddy. This just got real. I tell Sonny on the ride over to dinner. I tell Alena at dinner.

Let me make this point. It's important. This was not an imposter Robin Thicke. This was not an alien telling me this was Robin Thicke. This was Robin Thicke.

The next afternoon I call the assistant and introduce myself. He tells me Robin mentioned that I might call. He apologizes that he can't talk and asks if I can call back the next morning. Yes, I can.

I'm still trying to find the Studio where No Doubt is recording their album. I can go there now with the added confidence that I might soon be working with another musician. Things are moving fast.

Tom Matte

Ken has moved from his small one-bedroom apartment to a new place on Colorado Avenue. He shares it with some roommates I will never see. I'm supposed to meet him there and pick up some coke. He tells me it's right across from the motor vehicle department. Sonny drives me over to Ken's. Sonny is also straight edge. He doesn't know I'm picking up drugs. If he does, he never lets on. This is something we just don't talk about. I don't think he would approve. He is a smart guy, so he might have his suspicions, but he is also working for me so he never says anything.

Sonny pulls into the address Ken provided. I get out of the car and look across the street. WTF! I'm staring at a giant Interscope Records logo. Interscope Records is the music label for No Doubt and Gwen Stefani! This is their corporate office. Clearly another sign from the universe. I pick up my drugs and hurriedly get back into the limo.

I'm going to make a calling card for Gwen Stefani and leave it at the Interscope front desk. I spend the next hour putting together this letter/business card/perfume bottle. It looks like something a child would make. Words don't do it justice. If you saw it your eyes would burn. Not from the visual horror, but from the fumes of the perfume. To this day I'm thankful to the security team at the front desk who would not let me upstairs to the Interscope offices. Twenty years of meetings with corporate America, and I should know this. I do know this: It's an epic fail on so many levels. But a private epic fail that no one will know about but Sonny and me. I still need to find the recording studio.

If I'm going to be working for Robin Thicke and Gwen Stefani, then I need to find a semi-permanent place in L.A. I call a local real estate agent and tell her what I'm looking for. A house rental in the Beverly Hills area. What's my monthly budget? $15,000. She asks a few more questions and we set up a meeting for the following day. She will come prepared to show me a few houses. We need to spend half a day together.

We meet at a Starbucks on Colorado Avenue. I'm dressed like a guy who wants you to know I remix clothes for a living. I stand out from a crowd and I'm comfortable with the attention. Tatiana, the real estate agent, is the spitting image of Sandra Bullock. Close to the same age. People tell her this all the time. She was even approached for an autograph once. She is easy to talk to. She looked me up on LinkedIn and viewed my profile. I have not thought about social media in six months. I just don't care anymore. I should be thankful that my profile was optimized. We have some of the same connections at a big law firm. She mentions some people we both know from LinkedIn. I just agree with everything she says. I don't recognize a single name she brings up. I tell her I'm recently divorced and starting over with a new career. After twenty years in the advertising business, I want a change. I have a knack for design and fashion, so I just went for it. I tell her about my potential new clients. In her former life she worked on music videos. She has worked with Michael Jackson and some heavy hitters in the music industry. She has been around L.A. long enough to tell who is full of shit and who is legit. She thinks I'm worth her time. She doesn't come right out and say this, but it's easy to infer. We get in her Lexus and start my tour of possible Beverly Hills rentals.

I call Robin Thicke's assistant and we talk for a few minutes. He is professional and polite. He asks if I have a CD or a website so I can show him photos of my work. A fair question. I don't. I send him this email instead.

Tom Matte

Furqun,

My design style is very hard to articulate in words, but I will do my best. I take brands that work for the artist and remix them. The result is a look that is very distinctive! I have a vision for Robin that will compliment both his style and his sound. I have been a fan for years and it would be fun to work with him. I watched the most recent episode of Duets and I know his protégé was sent home. If the rules allow I could give him an edge over the other 3 celebrities. If not, I could work with everyone.

I know he is very busy, but if I can meet with you both for an hour, you will see why I can make sure all eyes are on his Duet team! Looking forward to your response.

Cheers,

Tom

I wait patiently for his reply.

I have been at the Chateau Marmont for about a week when the front desk calls and tells me they are going to be fully booked for the next few weeks, my room included. I either need to check out today or, if I like I could stay in one of the super deluxe suites on the second floor. It's $2,500 for the evening and it's only available for the one night. I tell her that sounds fine. Can they send up some staff to help move my things downstairs? In a few minutes they are moving my stuff to the new suite. I will need to give them big tips.

The suite is huge, about three times the size of my current room. It has a grand piano in the living area, a kitchen, and a private bedroom in the back. It has a balcony that overlooks the bar/restaurant area. This is nice. That evening Alena stops by with her new boyfriend, Kal. Kal and I don't exactly hit it off the first time we meet. Eventually we get along so well that he lets me sleep on the floor of his apartment.

While housekeeping is moving my stuff to the new suite, I call Sonny and tell him I can't afford his limo company prices any longer. Sonny has slowly moved from employee to kind-of-a-friend. He offers up his personal car for a dramatically discounted price.

My last night in the hotel, I get a call from the bank. I don't answer my phone. I never answer my phone. They leave a voicemail telling me I'm overdrawn on my account by a few thousand dollars. I wonder to myself if that's including this night's stay. There is a chance the hotel may have already run it through on my card. Either way I'm out of here in the morning.

For the first time since I left home, I start to think about money. Everything I had in the bank is gone. Everything. Hell, I'm even overdrawn. I'm not as worried as I should be for a number of reasons. The first is that I have some new job possibilities remixing clothes for musicians. I've been training and investing in this for the last six months. I can't fail. The second, and this is a big one, I have an eighteen-carat-gold Spanish coin that I purchased in St John. It's valued at $13,000 or $14,000. It came with a certificate showing its history. It can buy me some time until I get hired. The final reason that I'm not as worried as I should be is because my judgment is off. But you know this already.

Some part of my mind is becoming aware of what is going on with me in the real world. I'm starting to feel the psychological pressure of all the bad choices I've made. Not that they were really ever choices. I felt powerless over my thoughts and actions. Understanding my financial situation immediately puts more strain on my cognitive process. This additional pressure is not helpful for someone in my mental state. I go into survival mode.

Chapter 14

June 2012

I have a plan. I've decided to create a story so outrageous that it has to be true. If it can be true, then I can believe it. If I believe it, then I will be able to sell it with confidence. An idea with big slices of truth along with a few little lies. Or big scoops of lies with little sprinkles of truth. I need to get some kind of income until I sign on with one of the musicians. That could be months from now.

I will use the last six months of my personal life as a framework for the story. I start to think.

Looking back now, I can see this time in a more positive light. The fact that I'm knowingly creating these lies is actually a good thing. It means that I'm slowly regaining my ability to separate fantasy from reality. At least I know I'm lying! This may sound odd to you. I hope it does. Part of my brain is taking its first baby steps out of my psychosis while another part is going in deeper and deeper still. It makes for a shitty next few years.

Sonny packs all my seven suitcases in his small 1999 Honda civic. They barely leave room for me in the front seat. I actually complain the radio doesn't work. What a dick. We head over to some pawn shops in Melrose. After shopping around, I find one that has the best deals for purchasing gold. I get about $2,500 for the gold coin. I give Sonny $600. This means I have $1,900 to last me till I get some income. Not much.

We drive to the Ocean Lodge Motel in Santa Barbara. It's right across from the pier. It's affordable at about $140 a night. Then Sonny does something that takes a load off my mind: He offers to store six of my seven suitcases at his home. Great idea, Sonny. Thanks for the offer. This will make my getting around much easier. Now I have only one suitcase to lug around. He leaves me at the Ocean Lodge and goes home for the day.

I have nothing to do, so I decide to look for the studio where No Doubt is recording their new album. I don't realize that the Interscope Records corporate office is also in Santa Monica, a few miles away from the beach. With my limited knowledge of this area, I assume the studio will be near the pier or the huge shopping area near the beach. Somewhere near Third Street. I'm standing under the Santa Monica pier looking up at the sky. A guy walks up and says, "Can I help you find something?" I don't really pay much attention to him before I answer with a question: "Do you know where a recording studio might be around here?"

"I know of two. Follow me. I'm heading that way now."

I run to catch up to him. He has on an old beat-up bandana and long brown hair. He is wearing a snakeskin coat, brown T-shirt, jeans, and boots. He looks like he's in an '80s hair band and is about to go on stage. His age is a mystery: late thirties, early forties, maybe. He acts like he knows what he's doing. Within about a minute, I get the feeling that something is not right with this guy. It's just a hunch, but a strong one. He starts talking about all the bands that have recorded in the studio we are going to. It's only noon so they may not be there yet. He talks like he knows the guys who work at the studio. He uses their first names. He plays bass guitar. Been on a bunch of tours. Will probably go on the road again in the next few months. He'll see what turns up.

We are almost to the studio when he drops this little nugget: "I'm the love child of Nikki Sixx and Sharon Osbourne." It's certainly not out of the realm of possibilities. I just follow along with the conversation, while I'm starting to wonder who I've hooked up with. We finally arrive at the studio. It's near the shopping area and Third Street. He knocks on the door and a twenty-something kid answers the door.

"Hey, Jack," he says, looking at my companion. A good sign. He does know these guys. The kid invites us in and he and Jack go into the back. I stay in the lobby area looking at the gold records on the wall. After a few minutes, they are back.

"Sorry," the kid says, "they aren't recording here. Not sure where they could be. There are a number of studios in the area." I'm not sure what he means by "area." We leave with a couple of bottled waters. I tell Jack that I need to get back to my room, I've got stuff I need to do. He says the other studio isn't open now and they don't like it if he just shows up. We need to make an appointment.

On the way back to the motel, I start to notice a few more things about Jack. He says hello to virtually every person we pass. He also has a smell about him. It's not exactly offensive, but it's pushing the envelope. I think he's using some scent to cover another smell. It's working. Sort of. As I look closer at his face, I begin to see it's covered in a layer of dirt. I thought it was a tan. It's a tan with a layer of dirt over it. He's either homeless or has really bad personal hygiene by choice.

We are in front of my motel and I'm about to thank him for his help. I'm also going to give him $20 for his time. Before I can get the money out of my pocket, he points to my motel and asks if he can take a shower? Sure. As soon as we walk in the room, he heads to the bathroom and shuts the door. He takes a long shower. Thirty minutes. He asks to use my razor to trim his beard. Sure. He stays in the bathroom a long time.

I ask if he wants a new pair of pants. He is a few inches taller than me and has a bit of a stomach, but I have a pair with some stretch in the waist. I also give him a new shirt that I think would fit. I try to give him some shoes, but his feet are too big. He comes out of the bathroom in his new clothes, smelling like soap. Much better. I can tell he's grateful. I'm grateful I could help him. I hand him the $20. He thanks me, puts on his snakeskin jacket and boots, bundles up his old clothes and walks out the door. I can't help but smile thinking of a homeless guy walking around in brand new $300 jeans and a $200 shirt. I have so much more to learn.

The next day I meet my real estate agent for lunch at Shutters in Santa Monica. It's right on the beach. Afterwards we spend a few hours looking at houses in Beverly Hills. I'm still convinced money will come in and I'll be able to afford a $15,000 monthly rental. We see some beautiful houses. I decide on one in the Bird Street section of Hollywood Hills. I ask her to make a bid. The owner is asking for $21,000 a month. I don't care. I'll find the money. She will need to get some banking info on me now. We swing by her office and I do some paperwork. I'm having trouble writing. I can't even recognize my signature. I have poor handwriting to begin with, but this looks more like something somebody would write after a stroke. I notice this but shrug it off.

I've checked out of the Ocean Lodge after one day. I have to be careful with my money. I'm also spending it on drugs, which are not cheap. That same evening I grab my last suitcase and head over to the Beverly Hills Hotel. I ask Sonny to drop me off on a side street. He has no idea what I'm about to do. He is confused because he knows I have no money. I tell him Alena is here and she said I could stay with her for the night. Occasionally, limos park on this street if there is a big event. You can also get to the main hotel this way. The property has a number of bungalows on site as well. These look extremely cool. I've never seen the inside. That's about to change. I've come up with the bright idea of breaking into one of the rooms and spending the night. If it works tonight, then the sky's the limit. I'll have access to the hotel whenever I want.

I choose a bungalow in the farthest corner of the hotel property, an area that gets minimal walk-through traffic. It actually gets no walk-through traffic. If you walk down this path, then you are staying in one of the four bungalows I've chosen.

I walk up to the front desk and ask about the availability of one of the bungalow rooms. I even give the number I have in mind: 2121. I've scoped it out through the bathroom window. The window is only about five feet off the ground. It appeared to be empty. The check-in lady recognizes my face. She knows I've been here in the recent past. I tell her I checked out about a week ago to check in to the Chateau Marmont. Now I'm thinking about staying here again. Would she mind showing me the room before I make my decision? Of course I can see the room. As we walk toward the bungalow she tells me it doesn't appear to be booked in the near future, but that could change. She also says a lot of people like it back here for the additional privacy.

I follow her into the room. I look around approvingly. I head into the bathroom. I need to get a visual of the inside of the bathroom, especially the inside of the window. I want to make sure there are no alarms. I slide up the window in the bathroom and make a comment on how nice the breeze is. She just smiles. Waiting. I slide the window back down and turn around. I tell her the room is perfect. As we walk back to the lobby she asks if I will be checking in tonight. It's already 9 p.m. I tell her more than likely it will be tomorrow. Should I hold the room? No. I'm not 100 percent sure, let me sleep on it and get back to you tomorrow. Sounds good. I leave excited. This is going to be fun!

I go to the bar and get a drink. I need some liquid courage. I also do some coke. After a few minutes, I start walking toward the room. If I get caught, I'll just tell them I'm shit-faced and forgot my key ... and my room number ... and that I checked out a week ago. I still can't believe I'm going to go through with it. I walk up to the window and with my left elbow I slam the bottom part of the window as hard as I can. The wooden frame, not the glass. On the first try it worked! It slid off its tracks into the bathroom. I now have a gap my fingers can fit under so I can slide the window up. It moves with ease. I proceed to crawl through the window.

I look around the bathroom. Something is terribly wrong. Horribly wrong. There are four pairs of ladies shoes on the floor. There is jewelry laid out next to the sink. HOLY FUCK! I just broke into an occupied hotel room at the Beverly Hills Hotel. I need to get out of here fast. I have to put the window back in place and exit through the front door. It's the only way no one will know I was here. Window in place, I bolt out the front door.

I try to be as calm as possible as I walk toward the main hotel. My heart is racing. Am I so wasted that I can't remember what room I just toured? Am I dyslexic with numbers now? I need to find out. I turn around. As soon as I approach the bungalow door, it dawns on me what I did wrong. I was shown the room on the second floor! Directly above the room I broke into. How could I have made such a mistake? It doesn't matter. I need a place to sleep tonight. I climb the stairs. Using the exact same technique as I used on the window below, I break into the empty bungalow. No one is here. I can finally relax.

It's impossible for me to relax. My brain is on hyper alert. Every shadow that I see makes me jump. The only shadows are from the trees. I keep the lights off in the room. I have my headphones on but the music is low. I hear the lady below me get back a little after midnight. I want to go downstairs and compliment her on her shoe collection but think better of it. I start to relax a little. Every hour that goes by I get a little more secure in my stay. I listen to music and eventually fall asleep.

I wake up to the sound of a room service delivery cart outside the window. It must be for one of the other three rooms. The waiter is speaking Spanish to someone. I have no idea what they are talking about. I hear him walking up the stairs. There is no possible way he is going to knock on my door. He knocks on my door. I'm frozen in fear. He knocks again. I don't do anything. He'll have to go away eventually. The sound of another bungalow door opens. A voice yells up to the waiter. "Is that my breakfast?" Yes, Senor? He becomes aware of his mistake. They have a good-hearted chuckle about it. These back bungalows may be more private, but they sure as hell aren't quiet. I look out the bathroom window waiting for everything to calm down.

Before I leave, I place a half empty ice tea cup on the desk. It's still sweating from the ice melting inside. I leave it as a kind of calling card. It's a childish boast. Other than this, it will be impossible to tell that anyone was here.

Before I leave the grounds of the Beverly Hills Hotel, I take my suitcase and leave it on the side of one of the main walking paths. In plain view. I hid it in the bushes the night before. Far away from Room 2121. My plan is for a groundskeeper to tell security someone must have left a piece of luggage behind. From my experience I know they will keep it in storage till I claim it. I'm only going to leave it for a day or so. I have everything I need for another night's sleep in my backpack. I'm not going to do this again. It's too nerve racking.

Jesus Goes To Hollywood

Chapter 15

June 2012

I'm waiting at Ken's apartment for him to return with some coke. He will be back in thirty minutes, but his friend has let me in. While waiting we make small talk. I mention to him I'm looking for the studio where No Doubt is recording. I know it's in Santa Monica and I know what the front of the studio looks like. That's it. No name. No address. He wants to see the No Doubt website with the video. Maybe he can help. He knows this area pretty well. As soon as the video cuts from inside the studio to the façade, he taps my shoulder. It's right across the street, he says. Adjacent to the Interscope Corporate Office. He walks by it everyday on his way to work.

We take a short walk. A city block to be exact. There it is. The studio name is etched on the glass door. Finally! I thank him and he heads back to Ken's. I walk around the block a few times listening to music before I get up the nerve to knock. I want to make sure I come across like I know what I'm doing. I'm convinced I look decent enough. I need to sound confident. I doubt the person who answers the door will let me in, but at least I can find out some more information: specifically, can you give me the name of Gwen Stefani's business manager so I can secure a meeting?

I knock. In a few minutes a man answers the door. Total hipster. Mid twenties, beanie, and a waxed handlebar moustache. His name is Pierre. He is extremely helpful. They stopped recording months ago. He's not sure of her business manager's name. He wishes me luck, telling me this is a really hard business to break into. I'm figuring that out. He gives me the studio's phone number in case I have any other questions. I leave there somehow knowing this would happen. I'm running out of options and money.

I start walking toward the Santa Monica pier. It's about two miles away. A good distance. I need to think. The walk will do me good. City buses constantly pass in both directions. I notice them but don't pay any attention to them. Why would I need to pay attention to a bus schedule? I have Sonny.

I check back into the Ocean Lodge Motel. On the walk to the motel, I come up with an idea that will give me a place to stay and if it works, a credit card as well. As it will turn out, I'm a terrible con artist, the worst Frank Abagnale Jr. protégé ever.

Frank Abagnale Jr. is one of the most famous con artists in American history. By the time he was eighteen, he had worked as a doctor, a lawyer, and a co-pilot for Pan American Airlines, despite having no training in any of those things. His balls must have been huge. I'm surprised he could even walk. Steven Spielberg made a movie about his life starring Leonardo DiCaprio, *Catch Me If You Can.*

I call the Beverly Hills Hotel and make an appointment to meet with the general manager. The meeting is set up for tomorrow at 11 a.m. It's going to be a big day. I go through the story in my head again and again, making notes on my iPhone for a reference. I may need them in our meeting. I dress in the most conservative clothes I have, which is not very conservative. I can't recall exactly what I wore. I know it wasn't a suit or a tie.

I arrive at the Beverly Hills Hotel at 11 and tell the front desk I have a meeting with the general manager. Within five minutes a man comes out of a side office and introduces himself. He is an assistant manager. The general manager is tied up with other things. He hopes I understand. I don't. I'm pissed. But there is no turning back now.

The assistant manager is a tall, slim Frenchman in his late thirties with two first names that sound alike: Jacque Jacques. This irritates me. No matter how fast or slow I repeat his name in my head, it always sounds like *asshole*. His French accent might be considered charming if he wasn't so uptight. When he's talking to me, I get the feeling that he is actively squeezing his butt cheeks to make diamonds. Not that he shows any of this. He is smooth. No emotions. Dull. He is the opposite of French Jeeves. He is French Vanilla.

French Vanilla leads me to a conference room on the first floor. We sit across from each other at the end of a medium-size conference table. I jump right in.

"As you may know, I've been a guest of this hotel three separate times since the beginning of 2012. I stayed for a few days in January. I returned for a longer stay in April. And most recently I arrived in late May and stayed for a little over a week. Each time I was here, I was gathering information for a report I just recently submitted to my boss. Technically, he is your boss as well. I work directly for the Sultan of Brunei, whose Brunei Investment Agency owns a number of world-class hotels across Europe through the Dorchester Collection. The Beverly Hills Hotel is the crown jewel."

I pause for a moment to let this sink in. No reaction.

"I have known the Sultan since we were kids at boarding school. He is a generous man. But when he hears rumors that accountants and senior managers at his most prestigious hotel are stealing millions of dollars from the company, he is not so generous. He wants to get to the bottom of it.

"I found out about this last summer when I was spending some time with the Sultan in the islands. We check in with each other every few years. We usually just talk about old times, our families, and play billiards. He only half jokingly told me I should do some research for him. He knows I've run a small advertising agency in Atlanta for the last nineteen years and am familiar with all the moving parts of a business. He asked whether I could investigate this possible fraud for him. I told him that I wasn't convinced I could handle something this size. And he said, 'Tom, you must do this for me. But no one must know what we're doing except for my immediate advisors. If you succeed, I will give you 15 percent of any money we recover or you can prove was stolen from my businesses. I will make you a rich man.'

"I couldn't refuse him. I spent the rest of 2011 getting together a team of investigators and forensic accountants."

I look directly at French Vanilla. "I know you are not a part of this, Mr. Jacques. This is above your pay grade. This meeting was scheduled with the general manager, Mr. Jones. I am here to offer him a deal. Not my deal, of course;

this offer is directly from the Sultan to Mr. Jones. Please relate it to him directly. Let me be on the record as saying that it might be wiser for him to find some time to spend with me before he makes a decision.

"Here is the deal: Tell Mr. Jones he has two choices. The first: Cooperate with me fully. I will be spending the next few months or longer going through your books with my independent accounting team. I need unfettered access to everything. Bank statements included. Deposit slips. Transfer notes, etc. Any information that will assist me in recovering all the money stolen from the Sultan over the last ten years. I am in no position to guarantee that there will be no criminal prosecution. I'm here to give Mr. Jones a chance to make a wrong right."

I pause. "I see you are taking notes, Mr. Jacques. Please quote me on all of this. It's important he understands."

Then I continue. "The second option is that Mr. Jones can do nothing. I will leave here today and you won't see me again anytime soon. I don't know how long it will take for the Sultan to send his internal investigative team. It could be months. Perhaps years. Maybe he will even change his mind about my report.

"Tell Mr. Jones that if he does take this first offer, I will need a bungalow to work from as my home office. I will also need a bungalow for my assistant. Not only this, I will also need an American Express Black Card. One for my assistant as well."

I stop to let it all sink in. "I know this is a lot of information," I conclude. "Do you have any questions?"

For the first time in my fifteen-minute monologue, Mr. Jacques speaks.

"This is a great deal of information, Mr. Matte. As you said, I will need to check with the general manager before I can proceed. Do you want to wait here while I go talk with him?"

"No thanks," I say. "I will grab some lunch at the downstairs café. When I'm done we can discuss next steps back here in the conference room."

I go downstairs and order lunch. Thirty minutes later, on my way back to the conference room, I'm greeted at the top of the stairs by Mr. Jacques and two security guards. French Vanilla tells me that they will take their chances and do nothing. I give a slight smile and a very subtle head shake, the kind you give when the person gives an answer that you think is foolish. I pick up my suitcase that security has removed from storage and start walking to the valet section escorted by the security team. I'm walked past the valet area and down to the curb. I thank the security team for the escort. They both turn and leave without comment.

Well, I think to myself, maybe I should have only asked for one American Express Black Card. I call Sonny to pick me up. I need a ride.

Chapter 16

June 2012

    Sonny drops me by Ken's apartment. I spend my last few dollars on coke. Inside, a girl hanging with Ken is smoking meth. Her name is Nova. She's twenty-one and talks freely about how she stole a few thousand dollars from her mom's bank account a few months ago. I ask her how, thinking she is full of shit. She gives a surprisingly sophisticated answer. It includes impersonating her mom's voice, a fake email account, and a stolen Social Security number. I guess it could work. I wouldn't know. My first and only attempted criminal enterprise died on the vine about thirty minutes ago. I don't tell her this. I just listen. She gives me her phone number and tells me to call her if Ken isn't around or can't score. She can get anything I need. She is starting a drug-dealing business. When she makes $30,000, she is leaving LA. She can't stand living with her mother, and her dad is an asshole who left when she was a baby. She sees him from time to time, but they are estranged.

    Sonny knows I'm having money issues. He has no idea how bad. I now owe him about $1,200. If he is losing his patience, it's not showing. Over the last few months, I have given him twice this amount in tips. He thinks the money will come, like it always has. He takes me to a motel a few miles from his house. It's near LAX. It's a dump, but my options are running out. I check in and walk upstairs to my room. The rooms on each side of me are occupied. In one room is a couple yelling at each other. The other has a man pacing back and forth. His blinds are wide open. He doesn't care who sees him. My mind is racing. Something has to break for me. My real estate agent needs a photo I.D. of me. I sent one earlier but it's not clear enough. I take a photo with my phone and send another for her approval. "This will work. Let's talk tomorrow about the final steps so you can rent this property, Mr. Matte." Sounds good to me.

Somehow, I'm still hopeful money will come in. I sit down to write Robin Thicke's assistant one last email to see if I can get a meeting. If this doesn't work, I have nothing left. As I sit down at a filthy desk on a broken chair, I feel the most excruciating pain coming from the top of my foot. It feels like an alien has taken two pinchers and squeezed my nerve. I slap my foot and start instinctively itching the spot. On closer inspection, I realize it's a bed bug. They are everywhere. Those suckers hurt! God damn it! Well, there's nothing I can do about it now. This room was $35 cash. I have no money left. What did I expect? It takes me an hour to put this letter together. I send it at 1:41 a.m. It will be waiting when he check emails in the morning. I'm sure I will get a call for a meeting within the next twenty-four hours and money will start rolling in.

Furqun,

I have rethought how to describe the creative design process that I bring to traditional brands (from Sears to Prada). I know I said photos would be sent today and if this email does not articulate how I work, I will send some photos soon.

Think of it like this. I can walk into any store and buy 2 of the exact same outfits. Now imagine if I handed one to Robin and the other to Justin Timberlake. Without my input they would wear the clothes and look the same. (I have not seen a "who wore it better?" for guys. FYI- I can do this with women's clothes as well, but I digress.) WITH my design input I will remix the clothes and you would not be able to recognize that they were the same brands! (I know, right!!) Of course I may add a separate pair of shoes and a few other design elements. Now for the fun part...whatever look I pick (with the artists input-an absolute must!) I can keep up indefinitely. I have an endless supply of ideas, kind of like Robin's song writing skills, the hits just keep coming and coming!! I have a vision for Robin that must be discussed face to face. I also have a Vision for Paula Patton that would work for each of them individually as well as when they go to red carpet events as a hot couple. I have enough confidence in my skills that I can GUARANTEE that TMZ and ALL the press will be writing and filming them. Bloggers and the usual Internet trolls included. Just ask the staff at Beverly Hills Hotel and Chateau Marmont. They all know my style, whether they admit it or not! ANOTHER GUARANTEE, and I am just some 48 year old divorced guy from Atlanta Ga. Imagine what I can do with a super star...or a COUPLE of super stars. Haha.

I just put a bid in to lease the house at the top of Blue Jay Road (Right next door to Tyler Perry, coincidentally I live a few miles from him in Atlanta) Ideally; I could host a dinner for Robin and Paula. I would prefer just the creatives at this meeting as I will be sharing my ideas and I want

honest feedback, not suits bullshit! (Side note, I will not be sucking up to either of them and telling them all their choices work for my vision, however I will respect all the honest input that they provide) I love to collaborate with ALL talented creatives! If my bid goes through, the lease starts July 8th. If we want to move at a faster pace I would be happy to buy them dinner at the Polo Lounge.

Thanks for taking the time to read this email and please forward it to Robin.
As a reminder my number is 404-555-5555. He is welcome to call me anytime.

Cheers,

Tom Matte

    I get no reply the next day. I call and leave a message just to make sure he is checking emails. Nothing.
    I meet with Sonny for lunch. He pays. I tell him things are about to break and I will have money to pay him. His look is skeptical but hopeful. I ask him to take me to the Santa Monica Pier. I'm not sure why. He leaves me knowing I will be in touch. All I have left on me is my backpack and my cell phone with a charger. My backpack does contain a jacket if it gets cold. I spend the rest of the day walking toward Venice Beach and back to Santa Monica Beach. I don't know what to do. Eventually I get hungry so I go inside Shutters for dinner. Shutters is a resort on the Santa Monica Beach. I stayed here one night when I had money, I'm not exactly sure when. I order a steak and fries. Dessert too. The most expensive items on the menu. I tell the waiter I need to use the restroom and will be back in a moment. After using the restroom, I proceed out a side exit down to

the beach. I just dined and dashed, something I haven't done since I was a teenager. I need to eat. I have no idea how to survive without money. I have a full stomach now but still don't know where to go or what to do. I'm scared as hell too. I walk toward Venice Beach again. It's now about 1 in the morning and I'm exhausted. I have nowhere to sleep and there's no way I can stay up all night and wait until tomorrow to ... to do what? I have no idea what I'm going to do. I have no money. No friends. No place to stay. No family that I trust. No family that trusts me.

I walk into another five-star hotel on Santa Monica Beach. I stayed at this one as well when I was flush with cash. I even remember what floor the linen closet is on: the eleventh. I saw a cleaning lady exit from it on my previous stay. From the street entrance, I casually walk past the front desk and up to 11. I push the door open into a room filled with nothing but towels and sheets. I take two sheets off of the closest rack and stuff them in my backpack. I then take the elevator down to the ground floor and leave through the back entrance. I walk toward the darkest part of the beach, an area where there is no light from the resort hotels or apartments. I find a spot about a quarter mile from the Santa Monica Pier. I place one sheet on the sand so I don't have to sleep directly on the beach. I use the other as a cover so I can stay relatively warm. The beach gets cold at night, and the wind doesn't help. My jacket is the real lifesaver. I wrap my backpack around my wrist three times and use it as a pillow. It has my phone inside, the only lifeline to any kind of help. If it gets stolen, I'm not sure what I would do. I fall asleep listening to the ocean and watching the Ferris wheel lights on the Santa Monica pier. It's one of the most peaceful night sleeps I've ever had in my life.

I'm woken the next morning by a man driving up and down the beach in an ATV. He asks my name and if I have a place to stay. I tell him my name. He writes it down on a clipboard. He tells me I can't sleep on the beach and gives me a dollar so I can take the bus to a homeless shelter in another part of town. He drives off after I nod in understanding.

    A homeless shelter? Are you kidding me? I'm broke, but I'm certainly not homeless. Then it dawns on me. I am homeless. Christie got the house along with any assets when our divorce was finalized last month. I have nothing. I just pissed away $350,000 in six months. Now I have nothing. How could this have happened? What the fuck is wrong with me? High-functioning drug addicts know they need to keep the money flowing to feed their addiction, or what I like to call the beast. If I'm not in control, then my beast should be taking care of things. It needs to be fed to stay alive. My actions completely disregard the beast. If the beast was sending me warnings or messages, then I was ignoring them. If I'm not in control and the beast isn't in control, then who's in control? This logic helps me realize that something beyond my understanding is driving me. I need serious psychological help. I need professionals to get some answers. Drug addiction is the least of my worries. I hardly know what I will do from one moment to the next. I'm confused. I'm scared. At least I have enough cognitive function to take the steps that will get me the help I so desperately need.

Low Life

Chapter 17

June 2012

    I pull out my phone and call Sonny. "Sonny, please come get me. I need one last ride. I can't pay you today, but I will have your money soon." He picks me up within the hour. I ask him to take me to the UCLA Medical Center. I need to check into the psych ward. Something is wrong with my mind and I'm sure these guys will help me get to the bottom of it. I have a sliver of hope. On the way to the hospital, I call my real estate agent and leave her a voicemail message. I'm having some personal health issues and won't be able to rent the house. Sorry for wasting her time.

    Sonny leaves me at the hospital E.R. He has to go take care of a paying client. I tell him not to worry, I will be in touch after they check me out and tell me what's going on. I'm relieved that I will finally get some help. My family was right the whole time.

    The E.R. is slow on this Saturday morning. I give the lady behind the desk my insurance card. She tells me I'm covered for this E.R. visit. I'm quickly ushered into the back and asked a series of questions by a nurse.

In a nutshell, this is what I tell her:

I'm a successful businessman with a history of drug use. Especially cocaine. I left my advertising agency in January thinking my wife was cheating on me and stealing money from the company. I tried to burn my house down to get the attention of the authorities. Not sure how that would really help. I also T-boned a cop car at our local police department. I did this under the delusion my wife was having an affair with one of the deputies. I have been flying around the globe staying in five-star hotels and spending money on expensive clothes. I burned through $350,000 in six months. It's everything I had. I filed for a divorce but never showed up at the hearing. My ex-wife got everything. I have no money left. This is so much more than just about addiction to a substance. Something is going on in my brain that is causing me to make horrible decisions and believe ridiculous things. I really need you guys to help me out. Maybe you can scan my brain and see if I have a tumor or lesion. I don't know what else to do.

They run some tests and I eventually get to see a doctor. I tell her the same story, with an additional plea in my voice. You guys have to help me. Something is terribly wrong with my brain. She gives me the usual detached response you get from a doctor in any clinical setting. She does have one bit of good news. They can check me up to the psych ward on the fourth floor. This is one of the best psychiatric teaching hospitals in the country. They usually have a waiting list for people to get in. I'm lucky: Today they have an available room.

I'm ushered upstairs to the psych ward and go through the check-in process. They take your belts and shoelaces. It's a precaution so people don't hang themselves. They provide zip tie belts so your pants don't fall down. It's a clever solution. It could also be used as a fashion statement in the right circumstances. They don't give a shit about how your shoes fit. They offer slippers if you have a problem. Heavy duty socks really. They have a rubber grip on the bottom so you don't slip and fall on the marble floors. They also provide gowns to wear. They are ill fitting and made of paper with flimsy paper strings to hold them closed. No one's going to try to hang themselves with these things. They are surprisingly comfortable.

I meet with a doctor the next day. It's not really a meeting. He comes in my private room and asks me a few questions. I try to have a conversation with him, but it's no use. He might be in residency. He is probably a psychiatrist. It's hard to tell. I guess he knows my story from the other doctor and the nurse. After a short while, he leaves the room. A number of other people come in and out of my room as well. I have no idea why. I quickly learn the most important person to know is the nurse, all the nurses actually. The nurse on shift has all the power. A more senior doctor comes in my room and asks some more questions. He is the medical doctor. Making sure I don't detox. He runs some tests. Near the end of the first day, I'm invited to a meeting with all my doctors and nurses. Maybe a hospital administrator. I'm not really sure who's on the invite list. I know I have to be there. It's not like I have anything else to do, with my shoelaces being locked up and everything.

My music is also locked up. What is it about mental health and music?

We meet in a small conference room. It has only enough room for a conference table and chairs. The staff is huddled at one end of the conference table and I'm at the other end. They introduce themselves and tell me they will be monitoring me for my stay here at the UCLA Medical Center. It's an intimidating environment, everyone sitting around a table discussing your mental health. I'm not sure if it's intentional or not – the intimidation, I mean. If it's intentional, then they are a bunch of bullies. If it's unintentional, then it's thoughtless and stupid. Either way, I'm not impressed.

I'm not sure who the head honcho is. They are speaking to each other as much as to me. There is some kind of doctor-patient, doctor-administrator subtext going on. I'm taking this all in while trying to analyze the intelligence of the group as a whole and each individual person. I'm not afraid to speak up and ask for a brain scan. I'm convinced there has to be a physical reason for my erratic and psychotic behavior. I don't say it, but I'm sure it's some type of tumor or lesion. They don't exactly ignore my request as much as they dance around it. They are all very serious, which is obviously a good thing. They are not in any way rude. Occasionally they talk to each other like I'm not in the room. They are overly polite, like I'm a nut case and they don't want to say anything that will set me off. One of the doctors finally speaks up. They have a preliminary dual diagnoses: Bipolar Disorder and Addiction. "As we moderate you, we may have another opinion. Lets see how things go."

BI FUCKIN POLAR! That's the best you can do? I've destroyed my entire life. Walked away from my business. My wife. My children. My friends. And you geniuses think its Bipolar Disorder and Addiction? That's what I'm thinking, but I keep my cool and don't say a word. I just nod in agreement. OK. Let's see how things go. I can play this game too, assholes. I leave with a diagnosis of my own: My doctors are idiots. As I get to know them I may have another opinion, but for now this looks like the most likely diagnosis.

I meet a few other patients the first night. The Opera Singer and The Mayor. One sings opera professionally while the other is mayor of a California town. By the time I leave in five short days, I will be convinced the opera singer is truly a professional opera singer. The mayor I'm not so sure about. It's certainly possible. I can't begin to guess what their mental health issues are from the time we spend together. What matters was how good they were at Words With Friends. They have a bunch of board games lying around the lounge area. It gives the patients something to do between meds. The Mayor grabs the board on the first night and asks if anyone wants to play. The Opera Singer and I are both up for it.

With the recent invention of my word game Eugenius and my obsession with the alphabet, I'm convinced I'll be a shoo-in as winner. Wrong! These guys are good. The Mayor wins the first game, the Opera Singer the second. The words they use are impressive too. They both admit to loving scrabble and Words With Friends. I'm not a big fan of either, but I have a decent-size vocabulary. My mother was a writer and we would play word games as kids. Jotto was her favorite. I think the game is extinct now. Before I snapped, I was a constant reader. I would usually have a novel open next to my nightstand or a science book written for the laymen. The evening ends without a win for me. The Mayor and The Opera Singer are both better players than I am. They have a strategy they won't share and I can't seem to pick up. The next day I finally win a game.

I learn very quickly that many people in the psych ward are smart. Like, really smart. The kind of smart that can outthink you if you let your guard down or happen to be a doctor. A light bulb goes on in my head that the doctors have to gang up on the patients in the conference room so they can keep control of the situation. I still think they're idiots, but now I have a better understanding of why they're idiots.

I make a connection with a young man who has some kind of neuromuscular disease. The muscles in his face don't move, so you never know how he's feeling. His face is essentially paralyzed with one expression. Frozen in place. I think to myself at least it looks more like a smile than a frown. I can't begin to imagine how hard it would be to go through life without being understood or having the ability to show emotions with your face. He also never talks. I'm not sure if he can talk; in any case, he doesn't talk to me and I never see him talking to other patients. It makes sense that he ends up here.

He throws the Frisbee with the Mayor and me. We get thirty minutes twice a day outside. It's an area on the upper deck of the hospital, so there's not much room. Enough room to throw a tennis ball or Frisbee. Not enough room to guarantee it won't fly over the side onto the grass four stories below. At first we never intend for the ball or Frisbee to fly over the side, but it happens, and when it happens, the nurse gets pissed. After two visits outside we have figured this out. This of course amuses us. Now we start to do it on purpose. Not in the beginning of our thirty minutes because then we wouldn't have a Frisbee. We do it with about five minutes left of our time outside. It's an additional entertainment for what amounts to very boring days. Usually the Mayor makes the effortless toss over the side when the nurse's back is turned to us. We immediately act like a bunch of third-graders who are going to get in trouble by the teacher. Our young friend with the frozen face doesn't show any sign of amusement or emotion toward our behavior. The fact that he hangs out with us every day is a sign that he is somewhat onboard with our antics. Finally one day our frozen face friend tosses the Frisbee over the side himself. He sees the mischievous and jubilant reaction on our faces. I can only hope he can feel internally what we are showing externally. Sure it's juvenile and childish. So what? Nobody's getting hurt. We want to make a connection with him. The Mayor and I are so proud, like two older brothers who just talked their younger brother into a dare. We both point to him when the nurse asks who threw the Frisbee over the side. She curses at the three of us under her breath. We walk inside patting him on the back.

Maybe that story has more meaning if you know that the frozen face kid is in here for a violent offense. Court-ordered. He beat the shit out of another kid for making fun of him. He is constantly teased by his peers and ignored by his teachers. Peers is probably the wrong word. He has few friends. His whole young life he has been an outsider. Never invited to sleepovers. He just wants to fit in and be like everyone else. His mother is afraid he's going to do something one day that he regrets and can't take back. Of course these are all rumors. It's not like we are invited to his group doctor meeting. The Mayor and I both know this. We never talk to each other about it. Not once. We don't have to. We recognize one of our own.

Chapter 18

June-July 2012

I've been here only five days and will be hustled out tomorrow afternoon. My insurance was accepted, but for a limited number of days. I'm not sure how I feel about it. No sense getting pissed. They clearly can't do anything to help me. They need to put a diagnostic label on me so they can process the claim and get reimbursed by the insurance company. I'm sure it doesn't look good if you fill in an insurance claim with. "Not sure what's wrong with this one." Over the next few years, I will spend a good amount of time educating myself on mental health issues. The sad truth is our understanding of the brain is limited. Even with all the advancements that have been made in neuroscience research across the country and globally, we still know very little.

They have a social worker check me out and make sure I have a place to stay. I give them Alena's name. I give them Sonny as a contact too. I'm supplied a list of sober living homes and recovery centers in the LA area. I think a few more days in a structured rehab facility would help me. I'm just starting to realize the extent of my insanity, the apparent total collapse of the executive function area in my brain. I can't plan ahead, which is a big deal if you're trying to make it through life with any kind of control. I also miss having my headphones and music and the calming effect they provide. This and the absence of any mind-altering drugs keep me anxious much of the time. I'm always anxious now. Not the kind where people would notice, not fidgety. The kind when things just don't feel right. A murmuring discomfort. I can't imagine going through the rest of my life feeling this anxious every day. I still need some kind of help. I just can't get it here. A name jumps out at me on the list: Malibu Recovery. That sounds like the place for me.

If I'm going to make it to Malibu Recovery, I'm going to need a ride from Sonny. This is not going to happen. I've been taking advantage of his goodwill for too long, and he's had enough. My final ride with him will be from the UCLA Medical Center to a motel, directly across from the bedbug motel. Another dump. We arrive at the motel with some of my luggage. His wife meets us there with the rest of the luggage that he has been kind enough to store at his home. This is not a good sign. His wife explains to me that they can't help me anymore and I should go home to my family. My children still love me. They need me. "Please, Tom, go home to your family. We can't help you anymore." They pay for the room for one night and tell me I'm on my own. Sonny leaves.

I'm in shock again. Scared too. I need to think. The pressure to make decisions is overwhelming. I know my judgment is bad, but I have to get my shit together. I have to do something. I call Malibu Recovery and explain my situation. The owner knows the folks at the UCLA Medical Center and checks out my story. I ask if I can come up for an intake session. She tells me the price. I explain again how

I just spent all my money, but I was notified by my ex wife that I have about $23,000 in a 401(k) that I plan on cashing out. I forward her the email to let her know it's legitimate. It will take about thirty days to get the money. She tells me to come up to Malibu the following morning.

The only problem is I don't have any money. I literally have no cash. I'll figure it out in the morning. It has been a long stressful day. I try to sleep, but it's hard. I have my headphones in when I hear the sound of two women fighting outside my window. It's about 2 in the morning. I look outside and see them punching and slapping each other. I reflexively run out and get in between them. I try to keep them apart, but it's no use. They want to fuck each other up. Now they want to fuck me up too. Bad idea. I hear the sound of an approaching cop car and head back to my room. The two women continue to fight. They start arguing with the cops, threatening more violence. I'm watching from my window. I'm also pumped from the adrenaline rush. This place is fucked. I lie back on the bed and realize that something has happened to my headphones during the fight. I didn't take them off when I jumped in between the women. The sound is muffled, like a wire is loose. I spend the next hour trying to manipulate them so the sound is normal again. I do a pretty good job of it, but I know they're damaged.

The next morning I wake with one goal: to get a ride to Malibu Recovery. I decide to go through all my luggage to see if there is anything I can sell. I find a MacBook Air that has been open but never used. Still in the original box. Shit! This is worth a good bit of money. I head across the street to a gas station. I ask the owner if there is a pawn shop within walking distance. "No. What are you trying to sell?" I show him the computer. "How much do you want for it?"

$600. "I'll give you $200." Fine. I can't imagine the cab ride costing more than $200.

I'm not sure where I am in LA. It's near the airport. I call a cab company and tell them to send an SUV or a van. I have a lot of luggage. The ride to Malibu costs about $140. It should be half that price, but it's a Friday, with bumper-to-bumper traffic all the way.

Before I leave the motel, I run into one of the women from the previous night's fight. She doesn't recognize me. Or if she does she doesn't care. She asks me if I want some company. No thanks. "Are you gay?" No. "Well you fight like a faggot." I guess she recognized me.

Joan, the owner of Malibu Recovery, meets me as soon as my cab arrives. We place all my luggage in the garage. Away from the other residents. You never know what someone will try to smuggle into rehab. The recovery center is located in a residential home halfway up a mountain road a few miles from the beach. A beautiful home with a beautiful view. The bedrooms are modified to hold two or more guests. Other than this, it looks like any other big beautiful home in Malibu. You would never know it was a recovery center from driving by. Well, excluding the ambulances that would show up every other day for one of the patients who had trouble detoxing. Joan is very welcoming and shows a real kindness and understanding of addiction. She has been doing this for a long time and it shows.

I'm assigned a room right next to the nurse's station in the basement of the house, away from most of the other patients. I tell her about my anxiety and needing my music to relax. She tells me I can keep my headphones for music. She knows I have no Internet access or phone service because of the mountain location.

This will be my second week completely sober since the Antigua rehab. I'm not exhibiting any psychotic symptoms at all. I'm anxious, miserable, and lonely, but I don't see any imposter people. I'm not communicating with aliens or receiving messages from secret government agents. I'm starting to hurt again from the lack of family contact. Physically hurt. Ache with loss. I need to be clear, my mind is not better. Not yet. I still think Christie is running a private business empire, but I miss her anyway. I also miss my kids.

I have become hyper aware of my surroundings, but not paranoid. I notice things now. I notice more. My mind has shifted some of its attention to be aware of things that in the past I would have missed. Or noticed but dismissed. I have a greater scope of awareness. More information gets into my head. It's an unusual sensation, being aware that your mind has changed. It's not the kind of change when you study for a test and memorize the answers. Or even when you have an a-ha moment working on a math problem. That's normal thinking, normal brain use. This is more like something was turned on in my brain. A part of my brain that I didn't even know had an ON switch. Since it has been turned on, I have been using it as best I can. Or better said, it has been using me! My new brain and I, we are trying to understand each other. This is new for both of us, so there is going to be a learning curve. It sucks that it involves so much collateral damage. I don't have an instruction manual. There is so much more that will happen. New insights. But before I can receive the wisdom and understanding, I have to plod through so much more shit and suffering.

I'm bored most of the time, lonely and depressed the other times. I don't even want to pull out my drawings or my writing. I'm just not interested. I tell one of the other patients that I remix clothes for a living. She gives me a few of her older clothes to see what I can do with them. I do my best to make something for her, but I'm not impressed with my results. They look like shit, really. I'm just not inspired. I also realize that maybe I can't remix clothes for women. I really don't care anymore though.

    I meet with the rehab psychiatrist to discuss how I need the music to make me feel calm and less anxious. She is OK with me keeping my headphones. I also mention to her that while I'm listening to a song, I can increase or decrease the volume on my iPhone by just thinking about it. It happens all the time. I just started with this ability upon my arrival here. It happened by accident the first time, but now with focus I can do it on demand. I'm so sure of this ability that I show her. She sees the volume go up on the iPhone while the song is playing. She can also see that I'm not touching any of the control buttons on the phone. My hands are right there for her to see. She is not sure what to make of this and neither am I. It is very curious, though. I show one or two of the other patients and they seem impressed. How am I doing it? With my mind, but I have no idea how.

    I never again meet with the psychiatrist to follow up with my very specific but limited telekinetic skills. If I did I would have explained to her what I learned a few weeks after leaving the recovery center. My skills are actually a glitch in the damaged headphones. The lady at the Apple store said it happens quite a bit. The volume will turn up or down when the iPhone and headphones are moved a certain way. I leave the Apple store happy with this knowledge. I wish all the weird shit in my life had such simple explanations. I saw the movie *Carrie* and I know how things can get out of hand when you're angry. Telekinesis is a super power I can do without.

If this incident had happened just two months earlier, I'm sure I would have interpreted it in a different way. I wouldn't have even tried to look for a solution or explanation. I would have just run with it. This is a good sign.

Chapter 19

July 2012

Christie reaches out to me via email on July 6, 2012, while I'm still at the Malibu Recovery Center. She updates me on my 401(k) status. The pension administrator has to close out the entire plan and distribute the money to four of our former employees who paid into the program. It's all very official and takes some time.

Here is the email exchange. I'm clearly exhibiting some anger issues and taking them out on Christie. Said another way, I'm a self-absorbed asshole. My emails to Christie are cut and pasted exactly as I sent them. The typos are more than a function of careless spellcheck. Keep in mind that I'm clean and sober during these exchanges. I am also not yet on the street, but I know it's coming if the money doesn't arrive.

Tom,

I am attaching the documentation that you will need to move your 401k monies. Contact Jason if you have any questions.

Christie

Christie,
I need u to fill this out for me. i live on the fuckin street thanks

tom

Tom,

This is how you ask me to do something for you? I have struggled the past 7 months to survive. I get up every morning to face a barrage of lawyers, creditors and police not because I have done anything wrong, but because you have. This morning I got up at 5:30 because I had to drive to Marietta to meet with a bankruptcy lawyer. I have to decide how best to fight Wells Fargo, if I don't defend myself they will receive a default judgment that will put a lien on the house so that when I do finally find someone to buy the house they will get their $140,000 which will bankrupt me. Now lets recap your last 7 months, you have abandoned your family to sleep at the Ritz and the Plaza, travel from country to country, entered rehab after rehab, have a limo driver take you to Vegas where you gambled away $5,000, spent over $300,000 dollars to end up on the fuck'in street.

I have loved you all my life. I have taken care of you and your sons for the past 20 years. You promised that you would never leave the kids or me and you did. You need to get your life straightened out and start making up for the things you've done. I am not sure where your bottom is if it's not living on the streets but you once were a success with a family that loved you. I can't help you anymore. I have enough trouble keeping myself sane. I wake up everyday scared to death as a direct result of your addiction, your selfishness and your unwillingness to make the right choices.

I am sure you can go to a library, or email the document to someone to print so that you can get it filled out and faxed back to Jason.

Christie

Christie,

you could have ffilled out the form 5 times for the time it took you to write that. Please dp this last thing for me.
please. I am at bottom now... obviously

Tom

I follow with this email two minutes later:

Christie,

your lawyer is a crook too. He could worl out a deal with them but he is praying on your fears. total asshole

Tom

And finally this one two minutes after that:

Christie,

tell tou what, give me the lawyrrs number and I guaramtee i can get gim to change his tactic. o can help you with that... of you want it

Tom

Her response:

Tom,

Obviously you are still using drugs or if not you might want to use spell check. I can barely make out what you are writing. You say my lawyer is a crook, does it take one to know one? You say he is preying on my fears, I wouldn't have these fears if it weren't for you, you don't know anything about me or my situation anymore. I won't be a party to filling out your forms so that you can blow the money on renting a house in Malibu or using it for drugs. I am sure you can charm someone into filling out the forms for you.

Christie

I conclude the email exchange like this:

Christie,

I hope you are not this hateful to everyone. Dont contact me anymore unless you can be decent

Tom

I'm such an asshole! I'm not sure how I could ever have been such a world-class douche. But there it is, all the ugliness in black and white. I don't even acknowledge her pain and suffering. It's all me, me, me. She is suffering and I can't see it. Maybe I don't want to see it? Maybe I'm unable to see it? Her life sucks too. Maybe it's just too much for me to accept? I ruined our lives. Threw twenty years of hard work and a beautiful family under the bus. I'm not ready to accept that responsibility. No way. Christie is a hundred times stronger than I could ever be. That's clear. By the grace of God I will change. Become more compassionate and kinder. Not yet though. Still a dick for a few more months.

Like I said, I'm clean and sober during this exchange. Has my brain been permanently damaged from all the drugs? I need to find out. Things that used to be easy are hard. It takes real effort to do simple things. It's like the time I was in St. John earlier in the year. I stare at things and try to remember what they are used for. A phone, a television, a broom, etc. Eventually things come to me, but something isn't right.

Joan sees me struggling to fit in at the rehab. She can tell I'm not happy here. It's been a week and I haven't been able to come up with the money for my stay. I tell her there is an administrative issue that needs to be taken care of before I can get any of the 401(k) money. We have a talk in her office and find a sober living home that has agreed to take me in. They are much cheaper than a recovery center. She tells me to send her a check for my week's stay when and if I get my money. She is aware that she may never see a penny. She just wants me to get better. I thank her for her kindness and give her a hug. She hands me $100 cash to help pay for a cab to LA. I'm at a loss for words.

The Genesis sober living home is located in Cheviot Hills, California, a suburb of LA. It's about seven miles from the Crossroads Trading Company in Santa Monica, which will purchase pre-owned clothes, typically offering 15 to 20 percent of what they estimate the item will sell for. Example: Two months ago I bought a pair of $250 suede shoes. They offer $30 knowing they will price them at $150. It's a pawn shop for clothes. But they only buy trendy and/or name-brand clothes. I have seven suitcases of trendy and/or name-brand clothes. I will become very familiar with this store over the next two weeks while I'm living at the Genesis sober living home.

 The manager of Genesis interviews me about my situation. He will let me stay for two weeks. I can pay when my money is available. It's very generous of them. He tells me I can store all my seven suitcases in the attic. I'm starting to get annoyed at having to carry this stuff everywhere. It's a lot to lug around. Over the next two weeks, I will sell or give away five suitcases full of clothes. The home sleeps about twenty men at a time. When I stay there, they have about twelve guys. Most of them are in their early twenties or thirties. One guy is older than me but we rarely talk. I

have two roommates. One is a chef who I never see because of his work schedule. The other is a nice enough guy. I'm in no mental position to make any friends. I'm depressed. I want to go home to Christie and the kids. It's all I think about every day.

 There is nothing to do at the sober living home. They have a few AA meetings on the premises, but they expect you to find and go to local AA meeting with other members of the house. I learn quickly who leaves the house for AA meetings, who leaves the house for work, and who leaves the house to fuck around. After three days with an assigned sponsor, I get to leave on my own as long as I write down my daily schedule. I tell them I'm looking for a job. I'm not. I'm relapsing.

This is my typical day: Get up. Throw a few items of clothes in my backpack. Walk the half-mile to the bus station. Take the Pico Boulevard bus into Santa Monica, a seven-mile trip that can take forty-five minutes because of all the stops. Sell a few items of clothing at Crossroads. Take my $20 or $50 or $70 and call Ken. Remember Ken? Alena's ex boyfriend. He still gets me coke. He will sell me any quantity. It's a shitty deal. From a business perspective, I'm getting screwed every day. So what. This isn't business. This is addiction. I just want to feel any way other than the way I feel. I'm so depressed that I think about death every day now. I'm starting to comprehend all the damage I inflicted on my family. I'm filled with guilt. My life is unfixable, so what is the point in living? I take the bus to Ken's apartment and pick up my blow. Occasionally Nova is there. She is the girl who told me about starting a drug-dealing business. She starts to call me. Eventually I will be buying drugs from her instead of Ken. In October she will steal my car. But first I have to get back to Atlanta, to Christie and the boys ... and steal her car.

While I'm staying here, No Doubt releases their new single, *Settle Down*. I watch the video on a cracked iPad. Other than my phone, it's the only electronic item of value that I still have. The video director Sophie Muller uses bright colors to help set the tone. Gwen's right arm is covered in bracelets and ribbons. I like the way it looks. I should; I was wearing stuff on my wrist in a similar fashion just a month ago. Mine was not so over the top. But still. Sophie holds a shot on Gwen's watch for a second or more, obviously a sponsor of the video. It doesn't take anything away from the theme of the video. What is the theme? Something about a reunion and a party. What I do know is that in the beginning of the video all the band members are coming from different directions to a specific location. Some appear lost. Looking for directions.

A sample of the lyrics below. Of course they have nothing to do with me. How could they? I still find meaning in them. We do this all the time with music. It's what music is for. It's just another coincidence that they reference a person's brain and acting strange. It's also a coincidence that they are looking for someone. The bracelets. The bright colors. All coincidences.

> What's your twenty? (Do you copy?)
> Where's your brain? (Do you copy?)
> Checking in to check you out
> Concerned about your whereabouts
> Copy that (Do you copy?)
> You're acting strange (Do you copy?)
> So tell me what is going on
> So heavy I bet

I'm sitting on my bed one morning and Google "Bipolar Disorder." Hmmm. Interesting. OK, so maybe the doctors at the UCLA Medical Center are not complete idiots. My bad. Apparently doctors typically diagnose mental illness using descriptive psychiatry. From Wikipedia: Descriptive psychiatry is based on the study of observable symptoms and behavioral phenomena rather than underlying psychodynamic processes. In descriptive psychiatry, the clinical psychiatrist focuses on empirically observable behaviors and conditions, such as words spoken or actions taken.

Religious delusions. Flight of ideas. No insight into condition. Increased energy. Depression. Mania. Spending sprees. The list goes on. One research paper actually says, "Men may be festooned with ribbons and jewelry." This sentence jumps off the page for two reasons. The first is that it's 100 percent accurate. The second is that a researcher used the word festooned. It's not a word used in everyday conversation. My mother would have loved that word.

It's not that simple however. My symptoms could also be used for diagnoses of delusion disorder, psychotic episodes, and even schizoaffective disorder. I don't have to try and make the symptoms fit. I could have written them myself. I'm more and more accepting of the idea that my brain is a little fucked up. More than a little actually. It's all caps FUCKED UP!

There is some good news. I have no symptoms for OCD. Obsessive Compulsive Disorder is a disorder where people have to check things repeatedly. Things have to be a certain way. I go to breakfast with these new insights. I leave the bed unmade. I don't have OCD. I don't give a shit about a messy bed.

Chapter 20

July-August 2012

    The two weeks at Genesis Sober Living Home are the loneliest I can remember in my entire life. I'm depressed too, but the loneliness is what's killing me. My youngest son's birthday is July 21, and I'm not home. I missed Austin's in January, but I was too sick to feel the pain of missing it. This one hurts. It also hurts that he doesn't want to talk to me. Neither of them do.

    When training for triathlons, I would spend lots of time alone. I enjoyed training by myself. Three hours on the bike followed by an hour run. I loved being alone at those times. I never felt lonely. I was connected to something greater than myself. I had a family waiting for me at home. Not now. For now I'm on my own.

    The money from the 401(k) is finally deposited in my bank account on July 23. I have about $23,000. The first thing I do is pay for my two weeks at the sober living home. The second thing I do is leave the sober living home.

    I will go back to Atlanta after a few nights in LA. I check in to the Standard Hotel on Sunset Boulevard. These rooms are about $250 a night – a few miles and a world away from my recent motels. It feels good to have money again. Money equals freedom.

I'm jubilant when I arrive at the hotel. Real chatty. A pretty black woman checks me in. She asks why I'm in such a good mood. No reason. Life. We make small talk. I learn she is from Douglasville, Georgia, a small town about forty-five minutes west of Atlanta. I had a college girlfriend from Douglasville. For some reason I tell her this. I ask if she has a boyfriend. Yes, but we can see other people. She looks at me and smiles. I can feel my face turn red. I did not see that coming. She walks me up to the room and shows me around. She hands me the key and tells me to stop by at the front desk anytime I want to talk. Sounds great. I'm flattered by the attention.

I call Christie and tell her where I'm staying. I will buy a ticket in a few days so I can fly home and we can talk about the future. Whatever that means. What future? We talk almost every day I'm here. We miss each other, but so much time has passed the conversation is sometimes strained. We are both heartbroken. I ask her to tell me about the kids. Tell them I'll be home soon.

I'm not sure how she feels about me coming back to Atlanta. I know that not only have I broken her heart, I've lost her trust. She tells me that her girlfriends say she should be done with me. But I know she's a lot like her grandmother and looks for the good in everyone. Especially in me. We have a long history together. Not just a history of loving each other but a history of friendship, success, and children. I also know she's confused and scared. We both are. In the past we've always leaned on each other to figure life out. Maybe she's hopeful that somewhere deep down inside of me is the sane man she fell in love with. With Christie, once she loves you, she loves you for life. I'd like to think that's the reason she's agreed to let me see her and the boys again, but I doubt it. Fear makes you do crazy things. I should know, I'm an expert on doing crazy things.

Nova introduces me to her boyfriend, Sol. He is a twenty-something Korean-American. He has a car. No, he has access to a car. Not sure who owns it. I will hire him as a driver to get around from time to time. I spend enough time with both of them over the next few weeks to learn that they come from very different backgrounds than me. Nova smokes meth. Sol does too. I try it for the first time. Don't even try to begin to understand why. I don't know. It's similar to coke but different.

Nova tells me how she mostly hates her dad. She knows my oldest son is causing trouble at home. She tells me if I don't fix it he will hate me forever. I believe her. She almost died from some health problems when she was in high school. She was sick for a long time. She opens up to me about a lot of things. It's easy to tell she is looking at me as a pseudo father figure. But not exactly. There is something in her that is broken and that I can relate to. I'm broken too. One night, out of the blue, she says, "We can't save each other." It's a wise statement. It speaks to a part of her that is crying out to be saved. A part that wants to ask for help but doesn't really believe anyone will, even if she found the courage to ask. She is twenty-one or twenty-two, but in some ways still very much a child. I see this because I have two kids of my own. How could I help her anyway? How could she help me? I wish I knew. We both need something. What I need is back in Atlanta.

Nova also tells me more about her mother. Unfortunately, I will get to know her better when I come back in October. You would think that she was being overly protective of her daughter. After all, I'm some strange random old guy Nova just met. It has nothing to do with that. She sees me as an easy mark. It's true. I am an easy mark. Naïve. She helps Nova and Sol steal all my shit. She's not a nice person. It does help me understand Nova better.

I do a lot of drawing and writing while at the Standard Hotel. I create copious amounts of notes and illustrations. Some of the writings are absolutely insane. My thought process is all over the place. Partly fueled by drugs. Mostly fueled by the music. I still have my headphones in all the time. Nova hates it almost as much as Alena. I tell Sol and Nova about my experiences with synchronicity. First I need to explain synchronicity. I even set up a mini test. I want them to experience it firsthand. We put on a random playlist and they ask me any questions that come to mind. We record it on my iPhone. On playback, they will notice coincidences that can't be explained as simply random. For example: They ask my favorite color and the accompanying song lyric has the word "brown" at that exact moment. Same thing when they ask me where I'm from. The lyric "Atlanta" is sung at the perfect moment. Nova seems to be amazed while Sol just looks confused. One thing I know they're thinking: This guy is fucking weird. Maybe even crazy. They're also fascinated. Curious. Most importantly, I'm also a steady stream of income for them, helping me out as my taxi service and drug suppliers.

I check out of the Standard Hotel and move into the Hotel California right next to the Santa Monica Pier. I have a special connection to this place now. I'm not sure why or how to put it into words. Something happened to me when I slept on the beach that one night. Something spiritual.

I leave LA on August 4. I come back around October 10. I will spend the next two months trying to mend relationships with my now ex-wife and kids. I will do the best I can. It's a very uncomfortable time for all of us. I have blocked much of it out of my memory. Very few details of these two months remain. Certainly there are some good times with the kids. Not so much with Christie. I will live downstairs in the guest room for most of the time. Either that or stay at my dad's place like I did earlier in the year.

Synchronicity will be my biggest obsession over the next two months. I will tell my kids about it when I go back to Atlanta. They listen to me speak with a focused intensity. They look at me with a new set of eyes. Dad is not quite what he used to be. I'm not sure what they think about me when they are alone. Christie does her best to tell them things are going to be OK. They want to believe her.

One of the first things I do when I get back to Atlanta in August is make an appointment to get an MRI. I'm still convinced I have some kind of tumor or lesion that is influencing my judgment. The way I'm feeling. My psychotic thoughts. My anxiety. The second thing I do is apply for disability income with MetLife. I remember my disability policy on the flight back to Atlanta. This is exactly the kind of life-altering event that a disability policy is for. I congratulate myself for keeping the policy all these years. And for Christie continuing the payments through this year. We are both hopeful. It's a ray of light in the shit storm that has become our lives. I could receive an entire year's disability payment in one lump sum. I can't imagine ever working again, sitting through a business meeting. It has gotten to the point that I don't think I can do any job. I'm not comfortable around people anymore. They make me anxious. I have made monthly payments into a MetLife disability account since we started the advertising agency when I was twenty-nine. Twenty years with an average monthly payment of $129. That's almost $31,000 in total payments. I talk to one of the claims processors at MetLife. He is full of compassion and concern on the phone. I'm sure my claim will be approved. Not quite. I get a call and an email in a few days with a denial. When I was twenty-nine, I signed a document that excluded MetLife from any mental health claims. They are kind enough to remind me and email a copy of the page with my signature.

I'm not sure what to say to the guy. Then I find the words. "You fucking assholes!" He's heard it all before. "Twenty years of payments and you fuckers won't help me?" Nothing gets through. He ignores me of course. He is void of emotions. His job is to deny claims. Unless I can prove a physical disability, I'm fucked. I keep my fingers crossed that the MRI will come back with some kind of anomaly. I don't want a tumor of course. I would never wish a tumor on anyone, me included. The year before I left the agency, we had a loyal employee diagnosed with a brain tumor. They are ruthless, brutal on the victim and the family. I simply want to understand what has happened to me. From all the movies, TV shows, and books I've read, a tumor seems the most likely cause. If not a tumor, the MRI will show a brain lesion. Something tangible that can be removed. I want answers.

The MRI results come in and everything looks fine. Other than a deviated septum, the radiologist notices nothing unusual. This is a truly a blessing.

Fuck MetLife! Keep your money. Your advertising sucks too. Nothing personal of course, this is just my policy on handling corporate douchebags with no public face. No public face except Snoopy and that stupid Lucy character from the Peanuts cartoon. You know, the one who charges five cents for a psychiatric visit. Does anyone at MetLife realize the irony of having her as a spokesperson? Doubtful.

Chapter 21

August-September-October 2012

I'm doing my best to connect with my boys. They are glad to see me but also scared that I will do something crazy. They don't want me to hurt their mom anymore. I know this at a gut level. They don't have to tell me. They fight with each other all the time. It's painful to watch. I feel responsible. I am responsible. I don't know how to fix it, though. I need to fix me before I can even begin to think about fixing anyone else. We have become the poster child for a dysfunctional family. Not something Christie and I counted on when we started out. I mostly keep to myself in the downstairs guest room. Writing and drawing in my journals. I have a number of notebooks filled with peculiar poems. Thoughts. Ideas. Stories. Drawings of all kinds. Aliens included.

It's here that I start paying attention to numbers. Noticing patterns. Pattern repetition in everything I see. And hear. My mind starts to apply my new fascination with numbers to my childlike love of letters and the alphabet. Mixing and matching letters and numbers. I create sentences using numbers instead of letters. It's very basic cryptography. But it gets me thinking in new ways. I'm drawn into numbers the same way I was drawn into music and the alphabet. Numbers are a whole other universe that I will explore more next year. For me, understanding numbers is not the same as understanding mathematics. They are certainly related and obviously you couldn't have mathematics without numbers. Numbers on their own have a special beauty. Mathematics can sometimes miss the implicit beauty of numbers. It's a subtle point but important ... for me anyway.

I take Carson and a few of his friends to Dragon Con, a sci-fi/comic/fantasy convention in downtown Atlanta. It's held every year on Labor Day weekend. It's a fun day. Like before I went crazy.

The following day Christie answers a knock on our door. It's a parent from the neighborhood adjacent to ours. He's yelling hysterically about Carson and his friends threatening his daughter and her friends with a metal baton. I'm in another part of the house but I hear the commotion. I go to the door stand next to Christie and listen politely. When he is done speaking, I ask Christie to please go get Carson. This is very troubling. I would like to hear what Carson has to say. Christie looks at me with real concern in her eyes. I give her a look that tells her not to worry, I got this. Carson comes to the door and admits to showing these kids the batons they bought at Dragon Con: eight-inch metal batons that expand to about twenty-one inches. It's a serious piece of business. It could do real damage if your intention is to hurt someone. It's not a toy. Carson explains how they were showing the kids the baton. Not threatening. He doesn't say it, but the adults know. Carson and his friends were trying to look cool in front of the other kids. He apologizes to the dad and says it won't happen again. Carson goes back inside the house visibly upset. Christie follows him while I stay outside. I get a twenty-minute lecture from this guy about how kids should behave. I agree with him. The kids should never have been able to buy the batons at Dragon Con. I don't tell him I personally had to approve the purchases with the vendor. He finally leaves.

Carson comes into the bedroom where Christie and I are talking. He explains in more detail what took place. He wants us to understand that he would never hurt anyone. We already knew this. We tell him it was still a foolish thing to do. He doesn't disagree. He tells us that the dad is in everyone's business. Yelling at the neighborhood kids for walking on the grass instead of the sidewalk – that kind of thing. It's a moment that brings the family together. Uniting against a busybody neighbor. We have a laugh thinking about his expression if I told him I approved the purchases. Carson goes back to his room knowing we trust and believe him. Christie comments to me that she wishes I could act like this all the time. Handle family situations like I used to. That would be nice.

By the end of September, the $23,000 is gone. I have no idea where it went. Seriously. I have no recollection. Some of it was on hotels before I flew back to Atlanta. Maybe $5,000 total, a lot of money for lodging. That's just a guess. None of it was spent on clothes. I've moved past this obsession. Of course, some was spent on drugs – $2,000 maybe – and $1,000 on a first-class plane ticket. That still leaves another $16,000 gone. Maybe I gave it to Christie to help her pay some bills. I like to think so.

It's the first week of October. I have been home for two months. I have no direction or money. I decide to sell my Vintage pinball machine. The Monster Bash. It's in very good condition. I could sell it to a collector for $13,000, but that would require way too much thinking. It's too difficult. I sell it to a pinball company dealership for $7,500. Certain kinds of thinking are harder than others. I have no idea why. Planning things are nearly impossible. Abstract thinking is both easier and more comforting. I daydream of a better life for all of us with no plan how to get there.

I've stayed in touch with both Sol and Nova. Sometimes texting. Sometimes emailing. For a few weeks they go silent. Neither one returning my texts. Finally Sol responds. Nova is in jail. They got arrested for firing a gun in the city limits of LA. Something to that effect. He will make sure that Nova contacts me when she is released. You would think this would give me pause. Maybe these two should be avoided at all costs.

I'm using heavily again and starting to act erratic. Now that I'm paying attention, I can see a direct link to my drug use and increased psychotic thoughts. I'm not dangerous, just disconnected from any objective reality. Christie asks me to move out of the guest room. She doesn't care where I go, I just need to be gone. I have no problem with this suggestion. I head to the Ritz-Carlton Hotel in Buckhead. I need to spend some of the $7,500. I stay here till the money is almost gone, then head to my dad's place. He is traveling and won't be back for a few weeks.

As usual, my headphones are in and I'm listening to music. Scribbling madly in my notebooks. Waiting for instances of synchronicity. I have hours of recorded video on my phone. All containing unexplainable moments of synchronistic events.

A cop shows up at our house looking for me. I missed a court date. The court with the T-boned cop car, not the DUI. He asks Christie if she knows where I'm staying. She has no idea. I haven't told her my plans. I have no plans. She calls me and tells me the police are looking for me. My brain is not cool with this information. It triggers a wave of paranoia. This compounded with continued drug use for the last few days AND the fact that the words in my notebook are now animated. They are literally talking to me from the pages of my notebook. The letter B jumps off the page and we have a conversation. I don't recall the topic of discussion. I think to myself that talking letters are more associated with magic mushrooms than cocaine. In any case I have a few conversations with some other letters as well. Most of them are polite and thoughtful. Not the letter K. He can be rude. Other times he is completely silent.

I've been awake for forty-eight hours when I decide to drive back to LA. I sneak into our house in the middle of the night and pack for the cross-country drive. I take all my notebooks and drawings. I shove everything into one of those plastic waterproof Apple Store bags. I grab my work laptop that's been sitting here unused for most of the year. I throw some carefully chosen clothes into a suitcase and start my trip. I take Christie's Lexus. She let me borrow it to get me out of the house. I will be in LA in about thirty-five hours. I take a nap at a random gas station somewhere in Colorado. When I wake up I fill the Lexus with gas. It occurs to me that I need to check my bank account. I have about $150 dollars. This trip will turn out to be the worst idea in a year long history of very bad ideas. Not an easy list to top.

Life is about to kick me in the balls. When I'm bent over trying to catch my breath, it fucks me in the ass. No lube. Dry. It hurts. Did I bring this on myself? In some ways

I would say yes. Is it Karma? Hmmm. I've thought about it for a number of years.

As soon as I get to LA I call Sol and Nova. Sol asks me to come to his house and pick them up. No problem. I want to see them. He lives with his parents in Koreatown. Sometimes. Other times he sleeps in a group housing building on the other side of Koreatown. I think it's a place for kids that have no place to live. Sol tells me he is fighting with his sister. She is a few years older than him. The responsible sibling. She wants him out of the house permanently. He is violent and dangerous when he gets angry. His parents are afraid of him. I haven't seen this side of his personality. We hang out the first day I arrive in LA. We do drugs and sit at the beach. At the end of the day I drop them off in Koreatown. I drive around looking for a big enough parking lot where my car will go unnoticed. I don't have enough money for a motel. I save it for gas and food. I sleep in the car. It's not the most comfortable bed. It also gets cold at night.

Sol and Nova can tell I don't have as much money as I did last time I was here, but it's more money than they have. We meet a drug dealer in downtown LA's Skid Row. This is where the homeless line up tent after tent. They live here and sleep here. It's right in the middle of the city. It's a depressing place. I can't believe the number of homeless people in LA.

When I'm not with Sol and Nova, I drive into a used car dealership and try to sell the Lexus. Unless I have the title they aren't buying. I call Christie and ask her if she will send it to one of the dealerships. She tells me to go fuck myself. She also tells me that she finally has a buyer on our house. Her house. It has been for sale since the summer but there wasn't much interest. Now someone wants the house and wants to close by the end of October. She doesn't even ask me if I can come back to help. She has all but written me off. She actively hates my guts. This is too much for one family to have to go through.

Chapter 22

October 2012

    I've been in LA for about a week sleeping in my car. Driving aimlessly around. Sol invites me to shower and rest at his parent's house. It's in the middle of the day so his parents won't be home. His sister will also be at work. I jump at the chance for a shower and a bed. Even if it's just for a few hours. I let him and Nova take the Lexus while I stay at the house. I bring my laptop and suitcase in the house. I throw a load of clothes in the wash.

    I'm asleep on the bed in an upstairs room when his sister gets home from work. Who are you? I explain who I am and that Sol has my car. He will be back any minute. She doesn't want me in the house. She tells me to take my stuff and wait outside. She doesn't want me here. I call Sol but he doesn't answer. Neither does Nova. I leave my suitcase and laptop outside near the back door of the house, when Nova's mother shows up. She is wearing dark glasses that she never takes off. It's an overcast day. She doesn't want me to get a good look at her face. Nova has told me repeatedly how crazy her mother is. Now I get to see it firsthand. She asks what I'm doing here too. She starts telling me how weird it is that I'm hanging around a bunch of twenty-two-year-old kids. I nod my head in agreement. I admit that it is unusual. Not fully understanding at the time how bizarre it is. Looking back now, it's obvious. At the time, nothing was clear. She walks around to the back of her house and tells me I better stay at the front of the house until Sol and Nova get back. She says Sol's sister called her to come over and make sure I didn't start any trouble. I tell her I don't want any trouble. As soon as they get back I will take my car and leave. At some point in our conversation, I realize my suitcase is gone. Laptop included. I bang on the back door. His sister doesn't answer. Nova's mom says anyone could have grabbed it. Not true. An eight-foot-tall wooden fence surrounds the backyard. It's just a driveway with a garage, but it's private. It's designed to keep people out. This is not the best neighborhood.

  I think her mom has stolen my suitcase, but I can't figure out how. The simplest answer would be that Sol's sister helped. Pulled the suitcase back inside the house at some point. I don't believe this. She is too straightlaced and concerned about her parent's welfare. Something doesn't add up. I call Nova again, pissed as hell. She answers this time. "Your crazy mother is here and she has stolen my things. You better come pick me up." I'm no longer at the house. I'm pacing on the street. I tell Nova that I called the cops and reported a stolen car too. I didn't. Not yet. She tells me to chill out. We don't need any cops. She will be there in a minute and we can get my stuff back from her mom. A half-hour later, Sol and Nova show up. They have another couple with them in the backseat. I want them out of my car. Everyone needs to get out of my car. Once again, I have literally no money left or anything of value. I was considering pawning the laptop for a few hundred dollars.

I could have sold some of the clothes at Crossroads trading. I drop them off somewhere in Koreatown.

I still have my phone, thank God. It's my only connection to Christie and the kids. They don't want anything to do with me. At least I know I can call them. I also have my plastic Apple bag stuffed with all my notebooks and drawings. This gives me some comfort. I left them in the car when I went in Sol's house. Not that they are worth anything to anybody other than me.

Nova calls me the next day and tells me how I can get my stuff back. If her mom did take it then, she probably stored it at their house in Melrose. She wants me to pick up her and Sol so we can figure out a way to get them back. I pick them up late in the afternoon. We would need to go by the house when her mom is at work. This all seems a bit fishy to me, but I don't have many options. Sol is waving around a restraining order that his parents have taken out against him. He can't go home anymore or come within one hundred feet of his parents. If he does, he will go to jail. I look at the court order in amazement. I don't say anything. I start to wonder what he's capable of. I'm way out of my league when it comes to these two. These three if I'm including her mother. I live in the suburbs. I was raised in the suburbs. This shit doesn't happen in the suburbs. Or if it does, no one talks about it. It's kept in the shadows. We talk about our lawn service, mortgage rates, the weather.

This is not the suburbs. This is Nova's jungle. It's survival of the fittest. I'm not only unfit. I'm injured. I'm the gazelle that got swiped by the lion in the nature videos. I'm falling behind the rest of the herd. I'm the only one that doesn't know it yet. Not only am I injured, I'm asking the lions for help. This can't end well. This won't end well for me.

We drive to her mother's townhome the next day while she's at work. I wait in the driveway while Nova and Sol look for my suitcase in the house. Her mother always keeps the door locked and Nova doesn't have a key. She knows a side window that's usually unlatched. She will slip in this way. Once inside, she opens the front door for Sol. They spend about twenty minutes inside while I wait impatiently in the car. They come out heads shaking. It's not here. They are carrying a few other items, including a small Thomas Kinkade print. I don't say anything as we drive away.

A light goes off in my head. A very dim 40-watt light. They just took me on a "lick." A "lick" is a term they use for breaking and entering. Was I just used as a getaway vehicle for a petty crime? My lack of awareness is breathtaking in its completeness.

I drive them to a pawnshop so they can sell the stolen goods. Other than the Thomas Kinkade print, I haven't noticed what they lifted. Nova is going on about how she loved this painting when she was a kid. Her mother won't even notice it's missing. I play along. Not sure what to do. I could be wrong.

I pick up my iPhone and look back at a video I took of Sol when I first arrived back in LA. I drove a group of his friends up to the Hollywood Hills. It only plays for a few seconds. Sol puts his hands up to his eyes to cover them. He doesn't want to be videoed. Another kid makes a sign with his hands. Apparently it's a Korean gang sign. I'm the gazelle.

I drop them off somewhere in Koreatown. I drive to a police station on Olympic Boulevard. I walk inside and ask the officer on duty if someone can be arrested for driving to and unknowingly participating in a breaking and entering. His answer is no, not likely. I tell him I'm not 100 percent sure this is the case, but what if it were. He says the person wouldn't be arrested. I thank him for the information and leave. He has more important things to do.

I drive to Sol's parents' home. They are both there. First-generation Korean-Americans. They invite me in. I notice the clothes I left in the washing machine folded and sitting on a table. I put them in the car. I go back inside and ask them if they have seen my other suitcase and computer. No, sir. I raise my voice and start to yell. I think about how hard it must be for them with their youngest son. They need a restraining order to keep him away. My emotions swing between compassion and outrage. My oldest is acting out on the other side of the country. I leave them after I vent and realize they know nothing about my stolen property. I hate myself for how I acted.

For the first time in my life, I beg for money. I never imagined any kind of life scenario where this would happen. This was not in any five-year plan. Or ten-year plan. I'm hungry, I'm dirty and I look like an old drug addict. I tell people the truth. I'm stranded in LA and I want to get back to my family in Atlanta. Some kids stole all my money. I'm out of options. I point to my car with Georgia plates as proof of my story. Can you please help? I get a few dollars here and there. Occasionally I get a five-dollar bill. Not near enough to get back to Atlanta. Not even across the city. The most giving people are the ones who look like they can least afford it. The suits ignore me. I was once a suit. This is humbling.

I sleep in different hotel parking lots each night. Out-of-state plates are to be expected. No one will look in my car and see me sleeping. It's midnight and I get a call from Nova. She wants me to meet her. She has something to tell me. I'm reluctant at first. Where? Next to Tuscanos. A restaurant in Koreatown. It's closed when I arrive. Nova is standing alone in the parking lot. Next to the parking lot actually. On a dark side street. I pull up next to her and ask her what's wrong. She wants to tell me something. She opens the passenger door and sits down. She has a crush on me. She has for a while but didn't know how to tell me. This is total bullshit, I think, but what is her motive? Sol comes out from behind the restaurant. He asks Nova what's going on? She tells him we are talking and he should leave. He starts to get upset. Pretend upset. Like we have something going on. He is a terrible actor. I'm tired and over this bullshit. I have never been over something more in my life than I'm over these two kids. I tell Nova to get out of my car. I give Sol a hard look and he backs down. They don't go through with whatever plan they have. I drive down the dark side street and turn around. I drive past them. They are arguing on the side of the road. I look in my rearview mirror and watch Sol slip a gun into the waist of his pants.

I spend the next day alone. I talk to no one. I beg for money to eat. I'm always hungry. I'm lost. Other than my iPhone and my music, I'm alone. Thank God for my music.

On October 29 at about 7 in the evening, Nova calls. She is sorry about the other night. She was wasted and didn't mean anything. Does she want me to meet with her and Sol? They have money and drugs. Of course I go. I'm waiting for them at a gas station somewhere in Melrose. A lady walks by my car. I ask her if she could give me some money to get back to Atlanta. Anything would help. She tells me to pull up to one of the pumps and she will put ten dollars in the tank. I'm surprised by her generosity. For the first time in over a week I have over a quarter tank of gas in my car. This gives me a lift. Nova and Sol show up. They can tell I'm in a good mood. Nova asks to drive. Sure why not. Sol sits in the back. I'm in the front passenger seat. She asks if I'm thirsty. Yes, but I don't have any money. No problem, she will buy. She hands me a dollar and pulls into a convenience store directly across the street from where the lady bought my gas. She parks the car. I hop out and run inside for my drink. A sudden awareness hits me like a punch to the gut. I left my phone in the car. I left the car. I look outside and see Nova pulling out of the parking lot. Fuck me.

Chapter 23

October-November 2012

My mom used to say sometimes things go from bad to worse. Yeah, sometimes they do. I'm left with the clothes on my back. I also happen to be wearing a jacket. It's cool outside. On the inside of my jacket, I have my passport. It has been in this jacket for the last few months. I hadn't noticed until tonight.

I go back inside the gas station and ask the clerk to call the cops. Tell them some kids just stole my car. The cops arrive and I tell them a condensed version of events. I know who stole my car. I'm not sure exactly where they live but I can give you both names. The cop asks for some identification. I give him my passport. They run my name through the system. He tells me there is a warrant out for my arrest in Georgia. I ask if I'm going to jail. No. It's not worth anyone's time. Georgia won't spend the money to get me back there for a simple bench warrant. I've also broken no laws here. He does some paperwork and gives me a bunch of information about how to follow up with him in case the car turns up. I tell him I have no place to go tonight. He says he can't help me but there is a homeless shelter a few miles from here. He seems like a decent guy. He says it doesn't look good for a forty-nine-year-old to hang out with a couple of twenty-two-year-old kids. He says it in a tone like this: "I see a lot of fucked up shit on this job. You barely qualify as a blip on the radar. However, you are on the radar. You might want to get your shit together." He's right of course.

I start walking in the direction of the Pacific Ocean. My goal is the Santa Monica Pier. I will sleep on the beach tonight. In the morning I will figure out my next steps. It's about an eight-mile walk, maybe ten. It's only 8:30 in the evening. I will get there in about three hours.

I'm homeless. Bonafide homeless. No car to sleep in either. It may seem like a small difference. It's not. Sleeping in a car is safer than sleeping on the streets. If I remember our last conversation, Christie closed on selling her house and they will be moving to a townhome in about a week. I can't think about that now. I get to my beach around midnight. It's windy. It's twenty degrees colder than when I was here in June. I can't steal any sheets. I don't have a backpack to hide them in. I am not in that frame of mind anyway. I just want to survive the night. I feel beat down. Like never before in my life. I can't stay on the beach. It's too uncomfortable. I start walking around the mostly deserted streets of Santa Monica. Heading east on Wilshire Boulevard. There are a lot of homeless people in Santa Monica. An odd thought goes through my head. Why would you want to be homeless on Skid Row in downtown LA when you could be homeless here? I never ask anyone. It's just a thought.

I pass a glass door with a State Farm insurance logo. What luck! This is the company where Christie has her auto insurance. I will wait here until morning. As soon as they open I will have this agent call her agent. That's another thing we do in the suburbs; we have insurance agents. We have had this one for over fifteen years. I curl up in the doorway and try to sleep. I'll make sure I'm awake by first light. I doze on and off for a few restless hours. As soon as I see a little light I get up and start to look around. There is a Starbucks a few doors down. It's not very busy. I go inside to use the bathroom. It's warm inside. Nice. I decide to sit in the back for a minute on a soft chair. There is a black man about my age sitting next to me. He can tell I'm worried about something. He asks if I need any help. I tell him no thanks. I'm waiting for the insurance agency to open next door and they will help me. My car was stolen along with my phone and all my money. He says he thinks the insurance agency moved. I immediately go outside and look at the glass door. There is also a small piece of paper taped to the door. In little type: "We are moving to a new location on Wiltshire." Damn it. I turn around and the man is standing behind me. I can show you where it is if you like. I'm going that way. He is obviously from around here. That would be great. We start to walk toward the new location.

He tells me I should also apply for an EBT card. An Electronic Benefits Card. It will help me survive until I get on my feet. You can use it to buy food. The benefits office may even give you a place to sleep for two weeks if you've never applied for an EBT card before. I haven't.

He leaves me standing in front of the State Farm agent's new office. He wishes me luck. He tells me where the government building to apply for the EBT card is located. It's about another mile away straight down Wilshire. He describes the building. I can't miss it. I thank him for his help. In the thirty minutes I've known him, he has given me enough practical information to survive the next two weeks. The fact doesn't escape me that he was in a

Starbucks. Sitting. No coffee. It feels like he was sent to help me. A divine nudge in the right direction.

The State Farm agent calls Christie's agent and they get the ball rolling on an insurance claim. I ask her agent (my former agent) to please give me Christie's phone number so I can give her a heads-up on the situation out here. She wants to ask Christie first. She knows we're divorced. Christie tells her it's OK to give me her phone number. At least I have a way to reach her. No one remembers phone numbers anymore.

The EBT government building is exactly what you would expect it to be: big, ugly, busy. I go through a few levels of security and sign up to see a social worker. I'm not sure of the proper name for these guys. It's around noon when I arrive. My name will be called around 4. A slow, boring process. But what else do I have to do? What else can I do?

The social worker asks a bunch of questions about income and access to money. They want to make sure as best they can that I'm broke. I'm broke. They give me an EBT card with $220 credit on it. It needs to last me the entire month. Each month they will put another $220 on the card. When it's gone, it's gone. If you use it in a week, then you starve for the next three. They also have a box on the form that the social worker was supposed to check off. This box adds another $200 cash to your card after the first two weeks. Cash to be used anyway you need for survival. That's a total of $420 to get you through a month. Not much. If other people can make it work, then I should be able to make it work too.

One last question for me: Where do I want to stay? He hands me a piece of paper with a list of participating motels. Adams Garden Inn jumps off the page. I was at the Genesis Sober Living Home. I was Jesus for a little while. I almost turned into a demon and was dragged to hell. This fits the biblical theme. It's located near the corner of West Adams and South La Brea Avenue. He signs me up and tells me to go to another part of the building to check out. I now have my first EBT card. They also give me some bus tokens.

We read Yelp reviews in the suburbs. I discovered these reviews of the Adams Garden Inn when I was writing this book. I wanted to show Christie a Google Earth Image of the motel to give her a visual image of how rundown the place was. These reviews popped up when I entered the Adams Garden Inn name into Google. This will give you an idea of what other people have said about my new living situation.

Yelp: Review Number 1: Okay, seriously now pay attention to what I'm about to tell you. This is the WORST PLACE YOU CAN STAY IN LOS ANGELES. Nestled in a cozy corner of the West Adams neighborhood overlooking the pimps, hookers, dealers and liquor stores found in abundance all around you off of La Brea Blvd and filled with people staying from 14-30 days courtesy of the County of Los Angeles' General Relief housing vouchers the Adams garden Inn should be avoided at all costs. Sincerely, you're better off sleeping under a lifeguard tower on the beach.

Yelp: Review Number 2: I live around here and I can tell describe to you that NO ONE should live here because of the drug dealers, prostitutes, boppers, gang bangers, even the assistance bell was broke off. I even saw a clown faced hoe sniffing crack in the corner thinking I can't see her. Damn well I can! The building itself look like sh*t!

Yelp: Review Number 3: This place should not only be avoided but should be knocked down. The city is turning a blind eye on this place and does not care of the good neighbors around it. This is nothing but a place [where] the courts send all the people that the jails do not want. Stay away.

I take a bus from the EBT building to the corner of South La Brea and West Adams. The Adams Garden Inn is a quarter of a block away. I pass a bunch of liquor stores. I'm exhausted. I really need sleep. A man is standing behind a shaded bulletproof glass check-in window. You can barely see the outline of his face. I give him some information. He slides me a piece of paper to sign. He tells me I must sign it every day if I want to stay here. He hands me a key to the room. I walk up a spiral staircase to my room on the second floor. All the rooms face inward overlooking a concrete garden. I open the door. Wow. This place makes the bedbug motel look like the Ritz-Carlton. Not really, but you get the point. There is a twin bed in the middle of the room. It has a sheet thrown over it. There is a window air-conditioning unit from the 1970s. It doesn't work. There is a TV that also doesn't work. Somebody left his crack pipe in the bathroom. The bathroom? Let's just say it's dirty. I turn back to the bed and sit down. I finally feel the shock from the last twenty-four hours. It does not take long for this to have a negative effect on my already fragile mind. I lose it again in a big way. Alien conversations. Government agents following me. Imposter people. Paranoia. All my old symptoms come back. Fast.

You would think that I would fear the neighborhood and the residents. The crackheads. The felons. The gangbangers. I don't. Not even a little bit. This becomes my neighborhood. They become my people – for a short time anyway. What's the worst that could happen? I get shot or stabbed? Overdose? So what. I no longer fear death. In fact, part of me welcomes it. It would end my suffering.

I sleep for twelve hours straight. The next morning I notice the cockroaches that I missed the night before.

I use my EBT card for the first time the next morning to buy a cup of coffee and a snack at a corner gas station. I say hello to a security guard who is leaving the station. I know he is a security guard because it says it on the car he is walking toward. He says hello back and asks how I'm doing. Fine, thanks. You? Great. Have a nice day. This is the first full day at my new digs. I'm still relatively presentable. What I mean is that I don't look homeless. Disheveled? Yes. Homeless? Not quite.

Chapter 24

November 2012

    I head to my bank so I can borrow one of their phones to call Christie. I beg her to deposit enough money in my account so I can get a new phone. She reluctantly deposits a few hundred dollars. I get a new bank card too. I head to T-Mobile and purchase a new phone. New headphones too, of course. I get a cheap plan with limited Internet access. I need access to music. I can now watch music videos on YouTube or Vevo. No money for iTunes or Spotify.

    I also ask Christie to give me a few phone numbers of people who might help me. I call my sister first. She doesn't answer. She knows it's me, even though it's a new California phone number. I leave her a voicemail asking for money. She never calls back. I also call the friend from the West Coast who I called earlier in the year, the one who was worried about our kids. She answers the phone, not recognizing the phone number. I ask for money. She politely declines. I understand. I have one other call to make, an old friend who is living in LA. We were best buddies before I got married. We are still good friends, but distant. He may even let me stay at his place. I haven't seen him in years. I leave him a message. He never calls back. He's heard through the grapevine that I'm out of my mind and should be avoided at all costs.

I have no one left.

The phone is the only thing I own of any value. I keep it covered in my jacket when I walk around the neighborhood. I've learned to be cautious. There is enough money left in the account to buy some cheap notebooks and colored pencils. It gives me something to do during the day.

It's about a week later and I've gotten used to wearing the same clothes day after day. I run into the same security guard at the same gas station. Now I have a scraggly beard and obviously dirtier clothes. I'm drinking coffee. It's early evening. I'm standing in almost exactly the same location when I saw him the week before. I say hello again. He pauses before responding. This time he is not so friendly. "Get the fuck off this property!" he commands, walking toward me aggressively. "Don't be hanging around here! Get out of here!"

I'm not used to being treated like this by anyone. I tell him I'm just having a cup of coffee, I'll leave when I'm finished. "Why do you care where I drink my coffee?"

He's not used to being questioned from guys who look like me. He doesn't answer. He goes to his car and pulls out a wooden club. He starts walking toward me again. "I work for this company. It's my job to keep trash like you moving on." He wants to hit me. I just want my coffee. I ask him where the property ends. I'm amazed at my inner calm. I take a step onto the sidewalk.

"Can I drink it here?" I don't wait for an answer. I take another step into the street. "Can I drink my coffee here?" He starts to realize that I'm fucking with him. He's not sure what to do. Maybe he can't beat my ass when I'm off the property. Maybe the club is just for show. I have no idea with regard to the rules for beating up homeless people. Now I have an audience. A couple of locals are watching our exchange. There are always locals outside, hanging out. Always. Look at the crazy white guy. They are pointing at the security guard and laughing. He tells me if he sees me here again, I'm going to regret it. I believe him but I also don't care. I'm not a gazelle anymore. I'm a honey badger, and honey badger don't care. Honey badger don't give a shit. He gets in his car and drives off. The locals come over and tell me what an asshole he is, but to stay out of his way.

It doesn't take long for me to learn that my hardest day running an advertising agency was easier than my easiest day being homeless. Being homeless is the toughest job I will ever have. Unless you've experienced it, you have no idea. If you have been homeless and are reading this, then you probably have been blessed enough to have changed your life situation. If you're still homeless and are reading this, then I hope you find some relief soon. If you think homeless people are lazy, you are wrong. And ignorant.

The first few days I arrived here, almost every person I passed on the street asked me for a dollar. I told them I was broke. Finally they stop asking. Now they say hello. They watch me purchase items at the local grocery store. I have questions for the clerk about what I can use my EBT to purchase. They are strict on what you can and can't buy. Mostly food. Only certain types of food. You can't buy toothpaste or toothbrushes. No razors. No soap to clean yourself. I'm not sure I understand the logic. There really is no logic.

You can purchase ramen noodles. There is no microwave in my room to heat the water. No problem. I learned this little trick when I spent three days in jail for my

DUI. Turn the shower up as hot as it will go, place ramen noodles in plastic bowl, run shower water in bowl. Voila! Lukewarm, semi-cooked noodles. You won't see that on MasterChef.

There are a number of fast-food restaurants a few blocks away. You can use EBT at some of them. That's a plus.

There is a guy I see every day. He told me his name but I've forgotten it. He wears an Atlanta Falcons hat. He just got released from jail. I know this because he told me. He talks to me almost every day. Making his way over to me when he sees me leave the motel. He mumbles. I can't understand half of his words. The words I do understand don't mean anything to me because the other words are indiscernible. I've given up trying to comprehend him. I've learned to simply agree with everything he says. Eventually he will stop talking and I move on. He seems harmless enough.

Another guy I see almost everyday too. He showed up around the same time I did. Word is he just got out of jail as well. He's not harmless. He's dangerous. A big dude. I've seen him manhandle some people. He seems to get under everyone's skin in the neighborhood. I've watched people cross the street when they see him coming. He is to be avoided. You might call him a thug. One day I see him banging repeatedly on a door that houses a known crack dealer. I'm watching in fascination. This is not a good idea for so many reasons, the least of which is that you don't want to piss off your drug dealer. Finally a bald black man bursts out of the door, gun drawn, aiming it at this guy's head. The bald guy has a towel around his neck like he was just getting his head shaved. He still has shaving cream on the back of his neck. It's a scene right out of a gangster movie. But it's real life. I'm waiting for bullets to fly and a head to explode. Instead I watch a guy get pistol-whipped. There's blood everywhere. The drug dealer turns to go back inside, pissed he was interrupted while getting his head shaved. I have a feeling Pistol-whipped Guy will be back in jail soon. Or dead. No matter how much of a badass you are, there's always someone more dangerous.

These are the types of people I see every day.

My new drug dealer doesn't work out of a building. He cruises around on a mountain bike. He is in his early thirties and looks like Tyrese, the singer. His girlfriend resembles Whitney Houston. I will hang out with these two sometimes. I like their company. No one here asks personal questions. If they are curious about me, they don't show it. I'm not the only white person living in the neighborhood. There is one more, a thirty-something woman I see from time to time. Occasionally I see other white people. Always during the day. At night they disappear. This area is populated by African Americans, Latinos, Indians, and Asians. It's a melting pot, with two white people.

I'm smoking meth now. It's cheap and easy to get. It makes me crazy and paranoid. I spend an entire day riding the rail system and buses around downtown LA, trying to hide from the government satellites that are watching my every move again. No matter where I go, I can't escape their surveillance. For the first few hours this infuriates me. Then I come to accept it, knowing the government can only watch my actions. They don't have the technology to scan my thoughts. As I pointed out earlier, the aliens can scan my thoughts. They are patiently waiting for the right time to make their move. We amuse them. Especially the National Security Agency. Amateurs. Why would they use technology or even biotechnology when they can alter our human DNA and have us do virtually anything they desire.

One day I call my old partner at his new ad agency. He hasn't heard from me in over three years. I leave him a voicemail and tell him that he better be ready, I'm coming for him. Or somebody is coming for him. I'm not sure of the exact message. I call him again two days later and tell him I'm not kidding. If I recall correctly, I also tell him to save these voicemails. Make sure he lets the right people listen to them. He doesn't call me back. He is too busy thanking God he got away from me when he did.

Christie puts some more money in my bank account. I can now buy some personal hygiene supplies. I shower and shave. I put on new pants and a new shirt I purchased at a garage sale. They're new to me. I spend the rest on drugs.

Christie's birthday comes and goes. I don't call. I haven't called for a few days now. She moves into a new townhome. I've decided to kill myself. I call Christie to tell her. Tell the kids I love them, but I have no more hope and I don't know what to do. I'm sorry it has to end this way. She says that she hopes I don't kill myself because even though I'm crazy, the kids would be devastated.

She adds that she personally doesn't care what I do. She's also at work and doesn't want to talk. Her tone has changed. She is cold and detached. She has moved on. She hangs up on me while I'm still talking.

I get a call from Father Ed. The friend I was in the car with sixteen years ago when Christie told me she was pregnant. He's not just my friend, he's a friend of the family actually. We talk once or twice a year, usually around my birthday. He called Christie because my phone number has been disconnected. She explained how I've been acting over the course of the year. He is obviously concerned. He is a trained therapist as well as a Catholic priest. He is the priest who married Christie and me in 1997. He also baptized Austin. Carson's a heathen. We talk for a good twenty minutes. It's the most normal thing I've done in months. He wraps up the call by asking me if there is anything he can do to help. I tell him I have very limited funds. If he could put a few dollars into my checking account it would really help a great deal. I give him my account number hoping he will deposit some money. We hang up.

    That afternoon I go to an ATM machine to discover $1,000 in my checking account. I fall on my knees in tears. His timing is perfect. Last night was my final night at the Adams Garden Inn. Tonight I won't have to sleep on the street. I've been here for two weeks already. The $200 cash that was supposed to be deposited on my EBT card never materialized. I inspect a copy of the paperwork that the social worker filled out. He accidentally left a box unchecked, the box that said I needed the $200 cash. This was a careless mistake. He told me to expect the money in two weeks. I make a mental note to go back to the EBT building and work this out. $200 is a lot of money. But I don't have to go right away, I can use Ed's money to check into another motel. Any other motel. I get a room a few buildings away. I forget the rate. This is where my bicycling drug dealer stays sometimes. He is here tonight. I hook up and get high. I listen to music and write in my notebooks. I stay up for a few days. It's not the worst seventy-two hours of my life, if I'm to believe the aliens.

    The money runs out in less than two weeks. I call Father Ed and tell him I need his help. I don't know what to do, but I need to get out of LA. Christie won't let me go back to Atlanta. I'm not sure that's a good idea anyway. He buys me a ticket to New Jersey. He says I can stay with him until we figure things out. He has a number of connections at various psychiatric hospitals. Let's just get me to Jersey so I can see a psychiatrist. We can re-evaluate when I get here. I fly to Jersey the day after Thanksgiving.

I have been in LA for about forty-five days – the first twenty-one sleeping in my car, the next fourteen as a guest of the state housing voucher program, the last ten hopping between hotels on West Adams or South La Brea. Or sleeping on the sidewalk. I have no credit left on my EBT card. I haven't been on EBT a full month, so the next $220 credit hasn't yet been posted to my account. I never get the other $200 cash deposit on the card. So what. I'm leaving the state. I hope I'll never need this type of government assistance again. I'm damn sure glad it was there when I needed it.

I spend my last night in LA watching TV. Secret alien messages are being broadcast into my head as I try to enjoy an episode of *Modern Family*. I order a pizza for my Thanksgiving meal. This is the last warm night I will have for the next few weeks. New Jersey is cold this time of year.

Chapter 25

November-December 2012

    I arrive in New Jersey during Father Ed's busiest time of the year. He is organizing a major fund-raising event for Catholic Charities, a division of the Catholic church that helps the homeless, the hungry, and the poor, regardless of religious affiliation. How appropriate. Ed and I go back a long way. He was one of my teachers at Neumann Prep, the private Catholic high school I attended in New Jersey as a youth. He directed me in a few plays. After I graduated, we stayed in touch, calling each other every now and then, grabbing a drink together or seeing a Broadway play every few years. It's easy for me to be friends with him. He used to say he liked me because I don't take his position in the church as seriously as most of his parishioners. I tell him that I take his position very seriously. It's him that I don't take seriously. We have known each other for over thirty years. He lets me know that he has talked to Christie so he could better understand my condition and behavior. I tell him that's a good thing. I want him to know exactly how strange I've been behaving. At the end of the first day together, he comments that I'm certainly acting fine around him. It's true, I am. I don't even need my headphones. He sets me up in a spare bedroom.

The following day he goes to work and I relax at his condominium. Later he picks me up and we drive to the Catholic Charities fund-raiser. We spend a lot of time preparing for the night. Many things still need to get done. Christie ships my tuxedo to New Jersey so I can attend the event with Ed. I'm sure there is a joke in there somewhere.

The night of the fund-raiser, I'm seated next to a couple who have known Ed for almost as long as I have. They are nice folks, generous with both their time and money. They help with this event every year. We make the normal dinner conversation when you are forced to sit next to someone you don't know at an event like this. We talk about family, kids, jobs.

I mention that I just got back from California, leaving out virtually all the other details. They too happened to have recently returned from California. They visited their daughter, who is attending college in Santa Monica. I tell them how much I loved the area. They do as well. One thing did stick out that they found unusual. What's that? I asked. The number of homeless people. They ask me if I can guess how many homeless people there are in the Santa Monica area. Before I can answer, the husband tells me fifty thousand. Can you believe it? Fifty thousand homeless people in the Santa Monica area?

I don't say anything but I think to myself that it's actually closer to 49,999.

The one thing I do that I'm convinced Ed thinks is a little odd is write in my notebooks. When he leaves me at the condominium to go to work, I usually break them out and draw or doodle or play with some numbers. He doesn't comment on this activity. It's just a gut feeling. He makes an appointment for me to see a psychiatrist. This is a doctor

Ed has known for years. If I understand Ed correctly, he has been a mentor since Ed became a licensed therapist years ago.

We meet in his office, which is also his home. The first thing I notice about him is his age. He looks like he could have been a student of Sigmund Freud. I don't mean a student of his scholarly writings, I mean sitting in a lecture hall taking notes from the man himself. The next thing I notice is the Austrian or German accent. He will turn out to be a very knowledgeable and capable man. With over a hundred years in practice, you are bound to learn something.

I will visit him a few more times before I leave New Jersey and go back to Atlanta. He thinks I'm psychotic and prescribes anti-psychotic medications. I don't remember exactly what they were, but I hated them. They made me dizzy. He is the first doctor who uses the word psychotic directly to my face. It's an intentionally broad term and I'm sure he chose it for that reason. At this point in my journey I still think he is wrong, but I don't disagree with him. It will take a few months before I accept or mostly accept his diagnoses.

Ed makes a dinner reservation at an exclusive restaurant in Northern New Jersey. Members only. We are having a great time reminiscing about old times and my fellow classmates. He sees a few of them at his church on Sundays. Others he keeps in touch with like me. I start to feel normal. Somewhat normal, anyway. I'm not overly anxious. I allow myself a glimmer of hope that maybe my brain can adjust. Maybe I can fit into the world again. I start thinking about going back to Atlanta. Maybe if Ed gives it a green light and I'm under a doctor's supervision, Christie will take me back. Not for us. For the kids' sake. I start to think that I will do anything to make this right with the kids. They are the light that moves me forward.

There is another motivating factor that makes me want to get back to Atlanta. Ed keeps his thermostat set really low. You know how when it's cold outside and you leave a warm car to get to a warm house? With Ed's condo, it's just the opposite of that. You meander outside in the cold before you enter his freezer – I mean his home.

I spend a few hours at the Mall at Short Hills one afternoon. I'm alone. Ed has left town on business. I get an idea that some of the other shoppers are broadcasting messages directly into my head. Secretly communicating with me. I'm immediately aware that this is a ridiculous thought. It's just a thought. An idea. It might be true, but it's highly unlikely. No, it's probably impossible to communicate like this. No, it is impossible to communicate like this. It is the stuff of science fiction and movies. It's just an idea. A thought.

This is a very powerful moment for me. It marks yet another shift in my psyche. For the last year many of the bizarre or strange thoughts that entered my head I would consider real, or true. I'm now at a place where a bizarre thought or strange idea enters my mind and I don't have to act on it or believe it. My brain is developing a filter – the filter everyone possesses that I somehow damaged. It appears to be healing. I can play with my ideas now the same way a writer can play with his characters in a story, the same way an artist plays with the paint on his canvas. Unique ideas are my currency. For twenty years I made a living coming up with different and new ideas for my advertising clients.

Somehow, because of my drug use over the last twelve to eighteen months, all the ideas that popped into my head seemed real. I believed them to be real anyway. I couldn't separate fantasy from reality. Now as I sit here at the Short Hills mall, I'm aware of this distinction. I can entertain any outrages or insane thought imaginable. I begin to become acutely aware of how my mind is working, what I'm paying attention to. When the crazy thought pops into my head, I can flip it off or not, depending on my mind frame at the time.

Christie and I have a long talk. She thinks it would be good if I come to Atlanta and get some additional help. She needs help with the kids too. Especially Austin. He's constantly in trouble.

I thank Ed for saving my life. For all his help and generosity. Other than my parents, no one has ever been this generous to me in my life. I'm not sure he realizes the extent of his kindness, letting me take the few weeks to relax at his home and not worry about basic daily survival. He says we should all be this kind to each other. True.

I take a train to Atlanta, arriving on December 17, a week before Christmas. Christie and the kids have moved into a townhome a few miles from our old house. Everyone is anxious upon my arrival. I have a few days to settle in before the holiday. Christmas comes and goes. It is 100 percent better than the year before, but the kids are on edge that I will screw up somehow. The kids have a rhythm to their schedule that I don't want to interrupt. Carson is a freshman at Northview High School. He just got a small part in the school play *How To Succeed in Business Without Really Trying*. Ed had a copy of the 1967 film version. He lends it to me before I leave. Maybe Carson can watch it and pick up a few tips. When Christie and I see the play in April, it will be obvious that Carson studied the movie. He did pick up a few tips about how to represent his character on stage. Slowly, I will begin to win his trust back.

Austin has transferred to another school a few miles away, a school designated for kids who have fallen behind in their studies. He is now a junior. He is dabbling in drugs and getting in trouble. Just like his dad. The next year will be a difficult one for him. I crushed his world and he's found an escape to take away the pain: drugs.

Christie just wants my help. For the first sixteen years of our marriage, we had an unwritten rule: I make the money, she pays the bills and runs the house. She is wary, but after a few talks with Father Ed and information from the psychiatrist, she is hopeful. Maybe she is just grasping at straws.

It is exactly 365 days since I set the house on fire. It is December 29, 2012. So much has happened in twelve months. Our lives have been turned upside down. Other than the death of a loved one, I can't imagine a more Earth-shattering experience for a family. Before the next year begins, this one has to end. I wish I could say that 2012 was the worse year of my life. For Christie and the kids, that's probably the case. For me that title will be reserved for 2013. All the crazy and stupid things I did the previous year will catch up with me in 2013.

In fact, they catch up with me today. Christie and the boys are out of town, visiting her family in Virginia. I'm home alone. I get some coke and get high. It's not the same. This time I immediately start to hallucinate. This is the first time this has ever happened to me. I have four distinct visions, hallucinations. The first one is of the grim reaper, then a slot machine. Followed by an aerial view of a dinosaur's back and finally red blood cells traveling through my body. I am in awe of these illusions. I need to share them with someone. I call Christie and tell her what I can see in front of me as plain as day. She is obviously scared. She thinks I may do something dangerous like set the townhome on fire. Déjà vu all over again. She tells me she is calling the cops so they can check on me. That's OK by me. I'm relaxed. I throw away the rest of my drugs of course. This will be the very last time I do coke. I don't need it anymore. I don't want it anymore.

A cop arrives a few minutes later and knocks on the door. He says the station received a call from the homeowner that I might do something to hurt myself or someone else. I tell the officer that I don't plan on doing either. He asks for my ID and runs my name through the system. He comes back with his cuffs out. "There is a warrant for your arrest. I'm going to have to take you to jail." I'm compliant as he cuffs me and puts me in the back of the patrol car. I really don't think about what's happening to me. I'm still fascinated by my visions.

I will spend New Year's Eve in jail. I will spend the next twenty-one days in two different county jails. During 2013, I will spend almost ninety days in jail in separate counties. I will spend an additional sixty days under house arrest.

If 2012 is an earthquake, then 2103 is the rubble. And there is a fuck-ton of rubble to clean up.

Thug Life

Chapter 26

January 2013

    The Alpharetta City Jail is used as a short-term holding cell where you wait until it's your turn to go before a judge. Most inmates will be here for a week or less. On the night of my arrest, we are fed bologna sandwiches for dinner. They serve bologna sandwiches almost every night for dinner. The guards think it's amusing. Somehow it's funny that the only thing to eat is a bologna sandwich. I consider myself someone with a good sense of humor, but this doesn't make me laugh the way it does the guards. Maybe I'm hungry?

    On my second day they bring in a short young black man who looks about thirty years old. He's not happy to be here. The guards know him from previous incarcerations. He has some type of mental health issue, but I don't know exactly what it is. I can't put a name on it. If you spent any time with him you would understand what I'm talking about. I will come to find out nearly one out of every five people I meet in jail will have some kind of mental health issue. If we include addiction, it's closer to one out of three. Or maybe even half.

He is getting loud. Intentionally provoking the guards. Not physically, just verbally. His shirt is off. He is wearing nothing but a pair of jeans. The two guards run and grab their Tasers. I'm about to watch my first violent jailhouse confrontation. The first of many. This one is between the guards and an inmate. Usually it's between the inmates. As soon as they return, he starts in again, asking for a cigarette, daring them to tase him. It doesn't take much. The guards want to light this guy up. It's obvious to the few of us who are watching. He finally lunges at one of the guards. The Taser hits him square in the chest. It barely fazes him. The guard is about five feet away. Tased Guy keeps moving forward. He's walking like the Frankenstein monster now, slow and labored, but he will not be denied. The wires are hanging off his chest. I'm waiting for him to collapse. Everyone is, guards included. Nothing. He takes another step toward the guard. The second guard fires his Taser. He's got two Tasers sticking on his chest now. He takes another step, then another. Finally he collapses, his body convulsing on the floor. This all happens over the span of a few seconds.

Over the next year I'm going to see some pretty crazy things. Hear some pretty crazy stories. This sets the tone for what I should expect.

New Year's Eve in jail is exactly what you would think: a bunch of drunks ushered in and out. Most make bail in a few hours. We have a full house all night. It's loud and stupid. There are a few of us who have been here for more than two days. We will see the judge on Thursday, January 3. We would normally see him on Tuesday, but it's New Year's Day, a holiday.

By the time I get in front of the Johns Creek judge, I will agree to pretty much anything to be out of jail. For the record, this is the T-boned cop car incident, not the DUI and felony possession from Hall County. I have no lawyer. No legal advice. I don't realize it at the time, but this will come around to bite me in the ass. Hard. But for now, it doesn't even cross my mind. If it did, it wouldn't matter. I have no money. The prosecutor goes over my list of misdemeanor charges and her recommended sentence: forty-two months probation, fourteen days in jail – seven already served in Alpharetta, with another seven to be served in in Pelham, Georgia, four hours away in South Georgia. It's where many of the Atlanta suburban courts send their inmates. It's a shithole of a jail, an embarrassment to the state of Georgia. An inmate died here a few years ago due to lack of medical care. The GBI did an investigation. It was all over the news for a while. The jail got an all-clear, a nothing-to-see-here type of report. In 2015 many of these guards who let the inmate die will be charged with corruption under a separate GBI investigation.

I have to sign some documents and check some boxes, making sure I understand the conditions of my probation. The two conditions that will eventually cause me the biggest headaches are the following:

1. I understand that I will submit to a drug test by my probation officer.

2. I understand that I owe $48,456.57. (That's the value the city put on the flagpole and the police car I totaled.)

A third-party provider of probation service to the state will handle my probation. The company is called Judicial Correction Services. They collect my monthly restitution, court costs, and probation fees.

Jesus Goes To Hollywood

Before I officially start probation, I need to serve my remaining seven days in Pelham. Taser Guy and I are sentenced on the same day and ride to Pelham together in the transport van. To pass the time, I strike up a conversation. I ask him how it felt to get tased. Did it hurt? "Not really, it kind of felt like I was getting tickled." I'll keep that in the back of my mind in case I have to make a decision on getting tased or not. He asks if he can borrow a cigarette when we get to Pelham. I tell him I don't smoke.

Our van arrives late in the afternoon. I'm assigned to a large room that houses forty men. Bunk beds that are five wide and four across. At one end of the room is a small TV and some tables for cards or eating. At the other end are the toilets, the sinks, the showers. Actually shower; one is broken. There is a four-foot-high privacy wall that separates the toilets from the sleeping area. Attached to the privacy wall are the sinks. The sinks are facing the toilets. The toilets are facing the sleeping area. The sinks are so close to the toilets that if you wanted to, you could be taking a shit while you were washing your hands. At mealtime they come in with big bags of ice and drop them in the sinks. The same sinks you could wash your hands in while shitting. I never put ice in my drink. I can live with warm Kool-Aid.

There is an informal bathroom courtesy code at the jail. If you are approaching the toilet and someone is taking a shit, they typically yell, "Man down." The polite thing to do is turn around and let the man crap in privacy. As much privacy as possible. I quickly learn that some guys don't care who watches them shit. There is plenty of spare time to think about the shitting habits of men while you're in jail. While I'm certainly not a fan of taking a shit in front of someone, it's easier than wiping your ass in front of them. Go figure.

There are no bunks available the day I arrive. I'm given a cot by one of the guards. I stick it in the corner, near the TV. I'm up against the wall. The wall is seeping water. It's covered in a layer of fungus. There is no music in here. I spend most of my time reading. There are a few books inside left behind by inmates, mostly thrillers. The TV is on from 7 a.m. until midnight. The lights are always on too. At night they get turned down, but there is always some light.

I meet a seventeen-year-old black kid who is in here for wearing pants. The wrong pants. He was arrested in a nearby county because of his baggy jeans. It's a $50 fine, but he doesn't have the money to pay the court. I'm not sure how long he will serve for the minor offense of disorderly conduct. That's the charge they assign baggy pants. This seems racist to me. I tell him as much. The kids think so too. He also knows there is nothing he can do about it. I just want my seven days to be done.

They wake you up early the morning of your release date, those of us that have to drive back to Atlanta anyway. I hear my name called along with another inmate. We are moved to a temporary holding cell where we change out of the torn, orange jumpsuits that everyone wears and back into our civilian clothes.

While waiting in the holding cell, I hear the guards talking about how one of us has a "hold" for Hall County. A "hold" is where you have a warrant in another county. When I get back to Atlanta, they will put me back in the Alpharetta jail until a Hall County officer comes and gets me. It won't be until the next morning. I have no idea why they have a "hold" on me. The guards don't know either. They also don't care. I'm so freaked out by this. I call Christie as soon as I arrive at the Alpharetta jail. She also thought I would be home today. I ask her to please call the Hall County lawyer and find out what's going on.

Jesus Goes To Hollywood

It turns out the "hold" was for a warrant issued when I missed a pre-trial meeting in Hall County. This is the same warrant the California cop told me about in October, the same warrant that must have been flagged by the TSA as I was traveling last year. This warrant has been issued since March. My lawyer had no idea. He needs to get some papers in front of the judge. He's confident I will be released. It's just a matter of getting him to sign the papers.

The Hall County jail is everything Pelham is not. It has a military feel to it. It's bigger. Better funded. More inmates per pod – fifty-six to the one I'm assigned. I mentioned this earlier when I got the DUI. I'm back in the same cell. I'm so sick of being surrounded by inmates. The worst part is that I don't know when I'll be released. I should count my blessings. Some people sit in here for months before they get to see a judge. They don't have the money to bond out.

The TV in here is bigger too. There are daily fights over who controls the remote. *CSI* is popular. So is *House*. The most popular shows are the crime shows. This shouldn't come as a surprise to anyone. *Judge Judy* is big too.

One morning a Katy Perry movie starts playing on one of the channels. It's a documentary-style film following her Teenage Dream Tour across the States, including interviews with her family, friends, and fans. As soon as I hear this announcement I start waiting for someone to grab the remote and change the channel. Anyone: the Hispanic guys, the black guys, the skinheads, the rednecks – anyone. A minute passes. Then the next. Thirty minutes into the show and my mind will not allow itself to accept what's happening. There is no universe where fifty-six inmates are going to watch an entire Katy Perry movie.

Halfway through the film, I'm wondering who else wants to believe Katy's simple but powerful message: "Be yourself and you can do anything."

We watch the entire movie: two hours of Katy Perry on a January morning in the Hall County Jail. Apparently there is a universe where fifty-six inmates will watch a Katy Perry movie, and I'm living in it.

I'm finally released. I set up my pre-trial meeting. I make sure I know the date. I get back to the townhouse just in time for Austin's seventeenth birthday. We have the usual dinner and cake. He wants to be out with his friends partying. He avoids me like the plague. I don't know what to do. I know it's no use to force the issue. If anything will heal our relationship, it's going to require time.

Chapter 27

February-March 2013

I have my first meeting with my Johns Creek probation officer, Officer Smith. She is very formal. She likes rules. I have a feeling she doesn't like me. I know I don't like her. I'm too naïve to understand the power she has over me. The JCS probation office is a few miles from the Johns Creek Courthouse. I have to see them on a monthly basis. There are always people waiting in the reception area to see a probation officer. You hear talk about which ones are nice and which ones are assholes. The talk is that Officer Smith is a hardass. Austin will also get acquainted with Officer Smith in the coming year. He will have a completely different experience with her. He describes her as strict, but also understanding and decent. I wonder if we are talking about the same person.

I tell Officer Smith I have very little money. She tells me I owe $48,456.57. I don't have a job at the moment. "How much can you pay today?" $200. "It's not enough." Maybe $250. "You need to make sure that you bring $1,250 next month. That's how much your monthly restitution payment is calculated." It includes JCS fees and court costs.

I tell her it's just not possible. "Well, you better figure out a way to get it if you want to stay out of jail." I tell her State Farm, my insurance agency, has paid the majority of the claim to the police department. I have a letter from them at home with the exact amount paid. "Bring it to probation next month and I'll take a look at it."

This is the beginning of what will be a horrible relationship. A new type of pressure is weighing on me now: the pressure to get a job, get better, and make money. This is not helpful. I go deeper and deeper into depression.

Life at home only drives me deeper into an already dark hole. Austin tells Christie she is a fool for letting me back in their lives. He is waiting for me to do something crazy again. I embarrass him. He doesn't know how to deal with his emotions. There is no owner's manual for a broken home. Christie and I can't help. He doesn't want my help. I caused him all the pain. How could I possibly help? He fights with his brother everyday. The pent-up anger has to get out somehow. They take it out on each other. Carson feels the need to protect his mother from Austin. From me, if needed. From everything. Life is shit right now.

I need help. The whole family needs help. I'm desperate to be normal again. Is that even possible? I've never been "normal." Before, I was charmingly odd. Now I'm just flat-out crazy. Christie suggests I go see someone, like Father Ed suggested. It can't hurt.

I find a psychiatrist. She prescribes Wellbutrin for the depression and writes another prescription for Adderall. My ADHD is in overdrive. Adderall helps me focus. It helps my thinking. Both drugs will have an affect on me over the next few years. They are actively rewiring my brain in some way. I just don't know how. Music also helps with the rewiring. I'm still listening to music all the time. If I'm awake, my headphones are in my ears.

I've also picked up a new habit: using my fingers as if I'm playing a piano or a saxophone. I actually started noticing this in 2102. Now I do it daily. Multiple times a day. I only do it with my right hand. Strange. If I'm home, it looks like I'm manipulating an invisible puppet. If I'm out and the habit kicks in, I keep my hand down at my side. I know it looks peculiar. I still do it to this day. I'm not sure what function it serves. It fascinates me. Maybe, like the Wellbutrin, Adderall, and music, it calms my mind and helps me cope with the hurt I've caused my family.

The best thing about this entire year will be an introduction to mathematics and the history of mathematics. Christie gave me a Barnes and Nobles gift card for Christmas. I used it to purchase *The Joy of X: A Guided Tour of Mathematics from One to Infinity* by Steven Strogatz, a professor of mathematics at Cornell University.

Math becomes my new obsession. I channel my focus onto something that can actually be figured out. Something with concrete answers. It's a much better use of my mind. And my time.

As I immerse myself in math, I learn something very quickly. A writer can pose a mathematical problem a certain way and I'm lost as to an answer. However, another author can pose the same problem using different language, and it can be easier for me to understand and sometimes solve. This is a powerful observation. How you structure a math problem can help with how to answer the problem. Interesting. If you are a math major or math teacher, you know this. If you spent the last twenty years in marketing, this is a new and exciting discovery.

Without any teachers or professors to tell me I'm wasting my time, I have the luxury to make mistake after mistake. I'm self-directed and curious. I have nothing to prove to anybody but myself. I can spend eight hours a day doing the same simple operations over and over again.

I'm not sure why I have this new fascination with math. It must have something to do with my changing brain.

There is a term for very beautiful and difficult mathematical thinking and problem-solving: deep math. I stay mostly in the shallow end of the math pool. The shallow end is infinitely wide. Some of the greatest mathematicians in the world may have waded past a few gems. Or they weren't interested. If you can swim in the deep, why would you stay in the shallow end?

Occasionally I wish I could turn to a professor and ask a question, but I also know if this were a formal class I would have to do assigned work. I write my own lesson plans. Sometimes as soon as I write them, I disregard them and then bitch about the teacher.

Christie doesn't give a shit about my newfound fascination with math. She wants me to get a job. We have no money.

When I'm not working on math, I'm doing research on my hallucinations and visions. Even though I haven't used cocaine in months, I still have them. I learn the word *hypnagogic*. It's a waking dream state, the state you are in right before you fall asleep. It's an especially creative time for the brain. Many original ideas and works of literary art were created in this semi-dream state. I start to wonder if this can be related to my hallucinations. I read everything I can find on hypnagogic hallucinations.

I also purchase *The Creative Brain: The Science of Genius* by Nancy Andreeson. Turns out this new reading material will come in handy. I read it next month when I get sent back to jail.

Austin asks Christie to take him to lunch. We are both troubled by what he could possibly want to discuss. He has been getting in even more trouble lately. He constantly tells Christie that she is crazy for letting me back in their lives. He barely speaks to me. He actively hates me but takes it out on Christie. It seems ominous that he should ask her to lunch.

There is nothing for us to be worried about today. He just wants to come out as gay. He is a junior in high school now. We are both so proud that he has the courage to claim his identity. He thanks both of us for being such understanding parents. Neither of us are sure how else to handle this situation other than with love. I fucked up a lot of shit in recent years, but at least I can get this one right.

Chapter 28

April 2013

    I fail a drug test at the probation office. Officer Smith writes up a violation-of-probation report for the judge. She gives me a lecture on hanging out with the wrong crowd. I'm speechless. There is no crowd. I don't hang out. I don't go out. I sit at home, listen to music, and do math stuff. I do research on the Internet. I remind her of my doctor-prescribed medication. It's on file.

"It's not that," she says. "It's cocaine."

"NO WAY! Impossible."

"Tell it to the judge." People actually say that.

WTF! WTF! WTF! I leave the office shaking. I don't know what to do. I call Christie panicking. She doesn't know how to help. I have an idea. I will go to one of those drug-testing places right now and take another test. This will show the judge that it's a mistake. I'm in and out of the place in less than an hour. From my perspective, this is important. I wasted no time in getting a professional lab to analyze my urine. The test comes back negative for coke. I breathe easier now. Obviously there was a mistake at the probation office. She read the wrong line on the drug test.

A mistake anyone could make. The lab also sends the sample to another lab for deeper analyses of some kind. When that test comes back they will email me the results. Usually they match up with the office visit results. I take this as more good news. They will come back negative too.

I go to my Tuesday morning court date confident the judge will ...will what? I don't know. I know it won't be jail. How could it be? I didn't violate my probation. If anything, he could say I haven't been paying the full amount on the monthly restitution, the amount calculated by the probation company. He will understand. I've had some mental health issues. I'm trying to get back on my feet. It's been very hard for the entire family.

I'm nervous when I get up to speak in court. I explain the situation, or what I think might have happened. I don't accuse Officer Smith of lying. I've thought about that possibility over the last few days. She never showed me the test. I never asked for it. I was in too much shock. Even though we both actively dislike each other, I don't think she would lie about the results. It would be beneath her. I still believe that to this day. She made a mistake. She may have taken some pleasure in thinking I failed the test, but that's it.

I'm shaking when I talk. I hand over my lab test with the negative results for coke. I finish speaking. The judge holds up my lab test and, without a second thought or any pretense of giving a shit, gives me thirty days in jail. Starting immediately. I'm handcuffed by an officer and spend the rest of court in the inmate's section. Christie is there. We make eye contact. She knows I'm in distress. She's in distress too. She can't believe it either.

One more thing.

While I was speaking, the prosecutor stood up and interrupted me. I've never seen this man before today. He's angry when he speaks. He sounds like he has it in for me. Like it's somehow personal. I thank God he was not the original prosecutor on my case. He tells the judge that my seventy-nine-year-old father comes to the courthouse weekly, annoying the clerks and demanding more information regarding my restitution. This is true. My dad has tried to help me out. He feels the judgment is egregious. More importantly, it's already been paid by State Farm. He wants clarification, simple as that. They don't want to help. At all.

The staff at the Johns Creek Courthouse are not fans of Mr. Thomas Matte. He's the crazy asshole who knocked down their flagpole and T-boned one of their officer's cars last year. This will become even more apparent in the coming months. I have no representation or money to hire anyone. I'm an easy target. Mentally ill and poor. I'm not poor though; I'm broke. Big difference. And although I'm mentally ill now, I'm not going to stay that way.

They send me back to Pelham and the shithole jail in South Georgia. This time I get a bunk. I arrive on April 2. It has been about ninety days since I was here. I think I recognize one of the guys from January. He is in his late twenties. He is slow. Rumor has it that he was a great running back in high school. One night at a club someone slipped a drug in his drink. He hasn't been the same since. I don't know why he is here. For some reason he gets double portions at every meal.

I lay in bed the first week, bored. I don't shower. I start to stink. Even to me, I smell. I sniff my crotch and gag. I have one pair of underwear. The second week I receive a package from Christie with new boxers inside. They have stripes on the side. This is not allowed. I can have them when I leave. I tell the guard I'm wearing striped boxers now. "Those are fine. You arrived in those. New ones have to be white. Those are the rules." I spend the rest of my sentence trying to figure out the logic to this. It escapes me. The guard hands me a few books Christie sent. I start with *The Creative Brain: The Science of Genius.* I have something to do now. I take a shower and start to read.

I'm on my bunk reading. I get to the part in the book that explores the link between creativity and mental illness.

A light goes off in my head. A bright light. I'm a genius. Seriously. I'm a genius! There is no doubt in my mind.

This sudden awareness makes my day. I jump off my bunk and call Christie. I want to share the good news with her. I'm speaking fast. I can't get the words out fast enough. Here's my logic: There is no doubt that in the previous year I lost my mind. I had a serious mental breakdown. Walked away from my family and business. There is nothing normal about my mind, by any measure. Relentless psychotic thoughts and delusions. A complete disconnection from reality. My psychotic credentials are untouchable. If mental illness offered a degree, then I just graduated from every Ivy League school in the country, simultaneously. You can't disagree with this conclusion. You could, but you would look like a fool. Mental illness + Creativity = GENIUS. I'm a genius!

They say something is funny because it's true. This is so true that it's funny. I'm laughing now, like a mad scientist. What genius thing will I do to make me famous? I haven't decided yet. I'll figure that out later. I start thinking about who will play me in the inevitable movie made about my life. So many talented actors. Bradley Cooper? No, he's too good-looking. I'm leaning toward James Franco. Nice face. A little goofy. Smart. He's curious about things. An artist at heart. He's taller than me, but I bet he can play short. He has brown eyes. I have blue. Oh well, I'll figure that out later. He's perfect. I tell Christie all of this. She wants to know who will play her. Jennifer Lawrence of course. She's too young. We'll throw a few wrinkles on her. She has Christie's cheekbones and her sense of humor. She's smart too and doesn't take any shit. I can hear Christie smile through the phone.

Who's going to direct? She doesn't ask this. I think it. Maybe Scorsese or Tarantino or even Ron Howard. It's not a Spielberg film, that's for sure. Hmmm. Not sure. It will come to me.

I decide to spend the rest of my life as a genius. It feels good to finally have a plan. Most scientists, artists, and mathematicians are known for doing some genius-type shit first. Then they have a mental breakdown. I'll flip the script. Do it backwards. First have the mental breakdown and then become a genius. No one's ever done it like this before. The idea is genius. It's my first genius decision as a genius.

I wonder how much my decision to be a genius is influenced by the fact that I keep having these visions and hallucinations?

I fall asleep dreaming of the future. I also remind myself to look up the definition of the word humility when I get out of jail.

Chapter 29

April 2013

One day while I'm locked up at Pelham, a skinny white kid sits on the end of my bunk and asks if I want to learn how to build a meth lab. I have nothing on my calendar. Sure. Why not?

It's clear from the onset that he knows what he's talking about. He takes his time speaking. Goes over every step of the process and its importance to the end product. He is a gifted storyteller. Perhaps this was what it was like when the Greeks would listen to Homer recite *The Odyssey*. I don't ask any questions. I don't have to. He is thorough. Making sure to emphasize the steps that, if not followed properly, will blow up your trailer. This part is very important. You have to have the timing down perfectly. You don't want to get this part wrong. It's best not to make it while you're tweaking. That's when mistakes are made. I think back to an inmate in Hall County Jail. He was covered with burns. A meth lab explosion was the reason. A couple of other inmates start listening in. One of them asks if he can borrow my pen. I'm not taking notes, so I hand it over. The skinny kid speaks for another thirty minutes and answers questions from the inmates. Do you know how to make a portable meth lab? What are the best batteries to use? Does it even matter? Meth contains lithium you can somehow scrape from batteries. Drain cleaner too (the ammonia). He has answers for all the questions. This kid could have been a speaker at one of the CEO groups I was a member of in another life. He's smart. He knows it. He wanted to show off for the old white guy. The others are listening and taking notes, but he's talking to me.

The NCAA tournament is on TV. The TV is located in the upper corner of this shithole, about eight feet off the ground. The TV is as crappy as the rest of this place. Fuzzy picture. Tinted color, etc. If something exciting is on, like the Final Four, many inmates will stand in front of the screen and cheer for their favorite team. It can get heated. I'm sitting at one of the tables near the TV. Most of the inmates cheering today are black. In their late teens or early twenties. Some are cheering for Duke. Yelling at the TV. Telling the coach what play to call. Yelling at the athletes when they make a mistake. Typical fan interaction. One of the Duke players has the ball stolen by the opposing team. The kid yells at the TV, "You stupid rich white cracker!" He turns away from the TV, looks me right in the eye and says, "Not you, man. You're cool." I don't say anything. Just give him a look. It's all good.

So black people yell racist shit at the TV just like whites. They call us stupid, we call them stupid. They call us cracker, we call them something worse. The fact that he needed an economic variable as part of the insult doesn't escape me. Did I hear an additional element of contempt on the word "rich"? More so than on the words stupid or cracker? I think so. The class distinction is what I heard the loudest.

My nickname here is Old School. Or Pops. I prefer Old School. There are a few guys here around fifty. One or two guys may be older than me. I'm the oldest whitest guy here. Not in the entire jail, just in this shithole of a room. The old guys don't cause trouble. Usually.

I get to know an eighteen-year-old kid who recently graduated from the same high school my son attends. He's here for a minor drug offense. In my mind, we have developed a connection. When I first met him he mentions a young man who committed suicide his freshman year of high school. He talks about how it affected the entire school. The surrounding community too. This kid was a junior at the time. He tells me it affected everyone he knew. Some kids struggled with it for a long time. It doesn't make sense to him. The kid was good-looking, nice, and outgoing. He asks if I knew Will.

It has been about three years since Will's death and this kid is still dealing with it on some level. It's pretty clear to me anyway. He's right. It rocked the community. It rocked the school. Everyone went to Will's funeral. Everyone. It was like a funeral for a celebrity or rock star. This kid was loved. Is loved. His family too. All of them.

His parents have set up a foundation in his name: the "Will to Live" foundation. They help teens struggling with depression and other mental health issues. They help the families too.

Did I know Will? Yes I did. Our kids were in Scouts together back in the day. I remember him always having a smile on his face. I also remember thinking he looked like the kind of kid that could get in trouble and then talk his way out of it. He was the kind of kid adults like.

Will was also a guardian angel when I was on the road last year. Why would he be my guardian? I honestly don't know. I can only repeat what the kid said earlier. It affected the entire community, including me.

For me, Will's spirit would show up at the strangest times. When I needed a good idea. He helped with remixing some of my clothes. His spirit was with me when I was on St John. Usually when he was around, at some point, I would end up in tears. I tell him people miss him. He knows. He feels it. He tells me Austin will be OK. Carson too. He says what I need to hear.

He also actively teases me about my music. Particularly, my pop music collection on iTunes. It includes Britney Spears, the Pussycat Dolls, Katy Perry, Miley Cyrus and Christina Aguilera, to name a few. It's the kind of music some teenagers make fun of. Many adults too. Christie and the boys call me a "Pop Princess" when I get in the car and listen to my playlist. Will loved music too, just not this music. This teasing makes his spirit more real to me. He is playful. He is funny. He is kind. He is real. There is one fading memory where he had me laughing. I can't recall why, though. This memory is in my brain. I can see the folder, but I can't seem to access the entire file. It will come to me. I haven't seen Will's spirit in a few years, but I know he's around.

This exchange with the inmate who knew Will takes place some time during my first ten days at Pelham. I open up to this kid about my crazy past. (Not the guardian angel part. That would be too much.) Talking freely about losing my business and family. Losing my home. I don't give it a second thought. We just talk. That's not a good idea when you're in jail.

In about a week's time I will get into a fistfight with this kid. He steals some snacks from under my bed. I'm about to fall asleep and I see him reaching under my mattress. This takes balls. It's a bitch move. I'm pissed as hell. I jump up swinging. He's a good six inches taller than me. I land two punches in his gut. He falls down. He hits me in the face, but I don't feel anything. That's it. Fight's over. I start pacing. I'm hot but don't want to get the guard's attention. The snack thief is now sitting with about five other inmates, all in their late teens or twenties, eating my cookies. An older inmate comes over and tells me to let it go. I don't want to get another charge and extend my sentence, that's for damn sure. Now they are taunting me: Man, I'm full. Me too. Those cookies were good!

It's like an elementary school lunchroom but with gang members instead of fifth-graders. A calm passes over me. I go back to bed and lay down. The taunts continue. I keep quiet, waiting for them to shut up. They finally realize I'm not going to respond, so they start in on the kid that stole my food. The taunts are now directed at him. You got beat up by Pops. Old School fucked you up. He was sleeping. He woke up and knocked you on your ass. They recreate the fight. One inmate lies on his side pretending to sleep and then wakes up swinging wildly at the other inmate. They are laughing. Having a good time. Don't fuck with Old School! He wakes up swinging. I can't help but laugh with them. No one will steal cookies from me for the rest of my sentence. I've earned the respect of the strongest inmates.

Not really.

It's because I don't buy any more cookies.

One day there's a huge commotion next to the toilets. It doesn't take much to get inmates interested in something and hyped up. Most times it's something trivial or small. Not this time.

I hear a few DAMNS!!! A few WTFS!! I hear THAT AIN'T REAL!

This is what I hear to get me out of bed and walk to the toilets. I hear YOU GONNA HAVE TO GET A HOE FROM A GUARD AND BREAK THAT SHIT UP. THE BROOM AIN'T GONNA DO IT!

Now that's a curious statement. I have to see for myself. What happened? Did a rat climb through the pipes? Did someone stuff the toilet paper down the commode?

Neither. Remember the guy I told you about when I first arrived? The one who gets double portions at every meal? It turns out he has taken a shit. This is not just any shit. This is world-class. It's without a doubt the biggest human shit I've ever seen in my life. It's not a pile of shit. It's one giant turd. It's the size of a thermos. Bigger. Somewhere between a can of Raid and a roll of Bounty paper towels. I'm assuming the end in the water is tapered. I don't know though because I can't see it. What I do see is about 10 inches of shit above the water line, and it's not tapered! It just snapped off, so there's more where that came from.

If you were to sit on the toilet now, this man's shit would touch your ass. It's almost like, in the middle of shitting, he decided to get up and do something else. Or it's like the shit hit the bottom of the bowl and it didn't have anywhere to go so it started pushing him off the seat. I start to wonder. If he pushed harder, could he have cracked the porcelain? Wow. This is amazing.

I'm not sure what science this falls under. Chemistry, biology, material sciences?

The best that I can figure is this. Some chemicals in the jail food have mixed with the naturally occurring chemicals in this guy's stomach to create a new type of shit.

It's closer to a something you would find in a lab than it is to a normal shit.

I have to go sit down. This is too much. The other inmates are having serious discussions on how to get rid of it. There's no way it's going to flush. They've tried repeatedly. The broom handle hardly puts a dent in it. It doesn't come close to breaking it up. One inmate is insistent. "I'm telling you guys we need a garden hoe. It will cut it right in half! That's what we need! They got one in the tool shed. We need to do something!"

The real star of the show, the creator of this giant, is sitting in his usual spot. On a top bunk, back against the wall. Disinterested. He's watching the entire jail try to figure out a way to get rid of his shit.

The guards arrive and look in the bowl. You can see their eyes open in shock and wonderment when they realize what they are looking at. They glance up at the creator of this thing. They don't say anything. Silence. One of them finally speaks. He suggests cutting it in half with the garden hoe. Everyone eventually agrees on this course of action. In less than five minutes, the guards have chopped it up and flushed it down the toilet. Like it never existed.

Cell phones aren't allowed in jail. There is no digital image anywhere. No police report was written up.

But it did exist. I was there. I saw it with my own two eyes. Not just me. Forty inmates and a few guards. We know what we saw. That shit is legend.

Chapter 30

May 2013

    My thirty days are done. I walk home from the Johns Creek Courthouse, where the Pelham van drops us. No one is here to greet me so I have to walk. It's a little over a mile to the townhouse. I haven't shaved in a month. Showered and a haircut, but no shave. I look old. I feel old.

    I think about my upcoming court date in Hall County for the DUI and possession of an empty bag of coke. That's a tough break. It's a felony charge. I wonder how much time the judge will give me. I'm slowly changing inside. My soul too. Not just my brain. I turn on the local news. It's basically stories of people doing crazy things. It's sad and depressing. I have a level of compassion for others that I've never felt before.

    This news story sticks out in my head, a national story you may remember. A lady tries to drive her SUV into the ocean and drown her children. The reporter interviews a few locals. A typical interview comment goes something like: "She needs to get her kids taken away and sent to jail for a long time."

My thought is more like: Poor woman. Thank God she didn't succeed. Please get some help. I know you must be in so much pain. You love your kids. They love you too. Please don't send her to jail. It won't help. If anything, it will make it worse. My thoughts end with a plea to the Almighty for some kind of help for the person in trouble.

I'm slowly moving to the center left with my politics. I've always been socially liberal. Now I'm starting to look at money in a new way, from the perspective of a person who doesn't have any. Being broke helps me try to understand what it's like to be poor. I don't really want to know what it's like to be poor. Who the fuck wants to be poor?

Christie and I are having dinner one evening and I bring up my visions. This is a touchy subject because it reminds her of how crazy I was. I am. Up until now, she has always deflected the topic. When I talk like this, it makes her nervous. There has been enough time for her to see that I'm not acting crazy anymore, but that doesn't mean I won't act crazy again. I did before; I could do it again. I need to talk about the visions with someone. I'm well aware that to anyone else I would still sound crazy, but these visions are real and I need to share them. I try to explain how these "visions" are somehow different than my "thoughts." I do the best I can. I describe how the visions sometimes resemble a laser show. There are other types as well, but these are the most active. She is still skeptical but starting to get curious. I know this because she starts to ask questions. Questions that I can't answer. Not yet.

At the end of May, Austin gets arrested for having a grinder in his possession. A grinder is used for grinding marijuana so it burns more evenly. Christie and I have to pick him up at the Alpharetta jail. It's around midnight. We are sitting in the parking lot waiting for the bail bondsman to call. This is the same jail I was in for a few days. Christie sarcastically tells me I should be so proud, our oldest son is following in my footsteps. She is pissed. She is always pissed. There is so much dysfunction in the family right now. We can't seem to catch a break. She blames me. I also blame me. It doesn't really help anything but it feels better than thinking your kid is headed down the wrong road.

The bail bondsman calls. We can go inside and get Austin now. Christie gets out of the car and is about to shut the door when she asks, "Are you coming?" No. I hate that place. Too many bad memories. Plus I don't want to see any of the police or guards.

She slams the door shut without saying a word. She can add this to the list of reasons to hate me. It's a long list, but there's always room for one more reason.

This is Austin's first offense. He makes a plea deal with the Johns Creek prosecutor. He will get community service and six months' probation. This is how he meets Officer Smith at JCS probation.

Carson has an awards banquet at school, celebrating all the art programs. He tells Christie he doesn't want me to go. This hurts. I used to go to all his events, before the crazy. I am, however, slowly gaining his trust. We had a private laugh recently. It felt good. Like before. I know he wants to let me back in, but he's scared. He's very protective of his mother.

After the banquet, he rushes into the bedroom with an award: Best Actor, freshman class. He may not want me to go to the award show, but he certainly wants me to see his award. I'm proud and happy. The light in his eyes is real. Slowly I will mend this relationship. It's too valuable to let go. It will take time. Austin will take even longer.

Chapter 31

June-July 2013

I'm sentenced to ninety days in the Hall County jail. Plus, an additional four years and nine months probation. I listen to the prosecutor read my list of charges and thank God that I didn't hurt anyone. The judge seems fair. Thoughtful even. A big change from my last experience. I'm handcuffed and taken to the inmate section of the courthouse. I knew this was coming, but not the exact sentence. I'm sure if my lawyer wasn't a complete imbecile, I would have been better prepared.

I don't have to serve the entire ninety days. I've already served some time, and they have a two-for-one deal in Hall County. It's like a coupon at Chick-fil-A. But it's your life, not a chicken sandwich. It's a good deal and I'm thankful for it. Bottom line: I serve two weeks with the general population and then transfer for another two weeks on the work-release side. Upon release, I will be under house arrest for the next sixty days. I can live at home on the condition that I blow into a blood alcohol-measuring device. It's hooked up to a computer that the House Arrest Company monitors. It sounds an alarm when I have to blow into the machine. If you miss blowing, you get in big trouble. It goes off at random intervals. If I were drinking alcohol, it would register. I have nothing to worry about. I don't drink and I never leave the house. I miss it once during the sixty days, when I'm out back with my dog.

My first day in the Hall County jail, two inmates get in a fight next to my bunk. I'm facing the wall dozing and don't turn around to watch the fight. I know what's up. I couldn't care less. The guards come in and check all our knuckles, looking for cuts, scrapes, and blood. They manage to figure out who was fighting and drag them both out of the pod. Welcome back to jail. I keep to myself.

Even though I keep to myself, you can't help but overhear some jailhouse chatter. I listen in to a kid talking about his Nana. She killed a man in 1972. He was trying to get her to dance at a bar one night. He wouldn't take no for an answer. She finally told him to shut up and put a bullet in his head, right between the eyes. Dropped dead on the spot. She did twelve years in prison for murder. Now jump ahead a few decades. Nana has a few kids of her own. Her kids have kids. Everyone in the family knows Nana doesn't play games, grandkids included. This kid's mom tells him to stay away from Nana, she will get you in trouble. He sneaks over to her house from time to time and hangs out with her. Nana plays the slot machines at a busy corner mini-mart everyday. She talks to the owner. They become friends. Over time, Nana has learned when the five slot machines are filled with the most money. She also knows where the owner keeps the keys to the slot machines. And when the store is the slowest, when he will more than likely be alone. Nana has thought about this for a long time. If they time it right, they will clear $40,000 – a nice bit of money for fifteen minutes of work.

Does Nana's little grandbaby want to make $40,000? Hell yeah, he does. He recruits a friend. This is a two-man job. Nana has done her part. Everything goes as planned. Almost. No customers are at the mini-mart. The owner grabs the keys and starts unlocking the slot machines, emptying the cash into plastic bags. When he gets to the last machine, he drops the key. It slides under the thousand pound slot machine. Shit. They leave with the cash from four emptied slot machines.

They clear about $27,000. Nana is pissed. She was expecting $40,000. Her take was going to be $20,000 and $10,000 for each of the boys. Nana decides to use this as a teaching moment. She tells the boys that the money they left behind was part of their cut. She is still going to take $20,000 and they can split the $7,000. That's the end of it. Do you boys have a problem with that? No, Nana.

Her grandbaby just made $3,500 for a half hours' work. They get away with it too. No one is ever arrested for the crime. Obviously his most recent ventures weren't as successful; otherwise I wouldn't be overhearing this story.

I try to imagine my Nana taking out a suitor with a bullet. It's easier to imagine her taking us out for ice cream or pizza.

I'm moved over to the work-release side of the jail after two weeks. On the first day, I accidentally shut the door to my cell and it locks automatically. I'm now stuck inside the cell and have to call a guard from the intercom system. I tell the guard I'm sorry but I've locked myself in the room. She tells me we don't say sorry here, we apologize. I'm about to say sorry again and catch myself. I apologize instead. She says that's better and pushes a buzzer to unlock my door. I'm not sure why that's so important to this guard. Just another piece of Hall County jail etiquette I need to learn.

I share a room with an inmate named Puckett. He works fixing small engines at a local hardware store. He is gone from 8 until 5 every day. He is here for domestic violence. He has anger management issues. The judge has given him twelve months. He misses his kids but is happy to be away from his wife. He makes a joke about the jail not keeping him locked in but keeping her locked out. The guards know his wife as well. Sometimes she comes up to the gates of the jail and starts yelling, telling him what a loser he is. How is she supposed to take care of the kids by herself? She has anger management issues too. The guards stare and shake their heads. I realize he is not joking about her, not even a little bit.

I look for a job in Hall County as part of my work-release. Christie picks me up every day and we drive around from business to business applying for jobs. This is a complete waste of time, but at least I'm not sitting in jail all day. There is a chicken-processing plant around here somewhere. They're usually hiring. The inmates tell me it's easy to get a job there, but if I do get hired, don't plan on eating chicken again. It's a disgusting job.

I apply for a job at a local sheet metal manufacturer. They make paneling for the sides of something or other. If I'm hired, I have to stand over a piece of metal and drill holes all day long. I don't get hired and never get offered a job. None of the companies are looking for a marketing executive at the C suite level.

There is a guard who appears to have a learning disability. Apparently he has been working here for twenty years and has never been promoted. The other guards use him as their whipping boy. You don't want to get on his bad side. He can make your life hell and even get you sent back to the general population. I learn this my first week. I watched him dress down an inmate for thirty minutes. Inmates avoid him at all costs. Even making eye contact is a bad idea.

You have a few privileges on this side as well. Namely music. A radio or an iPod. No phones of course. I am listening to my iPod when dinner is announced over the intercom. My headphones are on so I don't hear anything and miss the announcement. A few minutes after, it occurs to me it's about dinnertime. I walk down to the open dining area. Everyone is eating. The food trays are outside our pod on the other side of a large steel door. I have to ask a guard for a meal. I'm really hungry or I would just let it go. I don't want any of the guards to know I exist. For the most part I've stayed under the radar. Only a week left before I'm released. The learning-disabled guard opens the door and asks why I didn't come down when dinner was called. I tell him I was listening to music. He screams and yells at me for twenty minutes, repeating over and over how this is not a private resort. I apologize. He eventually lets me eat.

I'm finally released on July 11. I've spent New Year's Eve and July the Fourth in jail. I'm now under house arrest for the next sixty days. I'm also on probation in two separate counties. I'm emotionally beat up by all that happened. I'm suicidal. Not just: *I wish I were dead* – that's an abstract idea of suicide. Now I'm thinking about how I'll kill myself. Probably hanging. I look in my closet and choose the tie. The ceiling isn't high enough. I know that if I die, I can't watch any more of Carson's plays. I won't ever hear Austin play his keyboard again. This gives me pause. Maybe tomorrow.

I've never felt this darkness, this hopelessness. It's like nothing else. I can never make things better. I'm a horrible father and ex-husband. I'm a horrible person. I can't imagine being better. What is "better"? I don't want to do anything. The thought of interacting with another human being is absurd. I have nothing to say to anyone. I can't imagine trying to engage in any meaningful discussion with anyone about anything. The thought of a job is laughable. I want it to stop. The pain. The misery. The emptiness. I shut my eyes and have these amazing visions. Constantly. But they aren't helping me now. They don't make me want to live. I have some strange new gift, but I don't know how to use it or what it is. Not only that, but it still points to me being crazy. No sane person has constant hallucinations. It can't be a good thing. The way I feel now, it's not a good thing. It's freakish and crazy and I'm tired of being both of those things.

One afternoon I have an out-of-body experience. I'm a political prisoner on another planet in a distant solar system. I'm being dragged to my execution. I'm terrified and afraid. I'm thrown on my knees in front of the ruler of this planet. Fear rips through me as I wait for death. Then nothing. It's over. I was just executed on another planet and now I'm back in this body. It's a mind-blowing experience for a number of reasons. Most of all is that it seemed so real. I'm still depressed, but after being executed on another planet, something in me was freed. I stop thinking about suicide and start thinking about other things. Life. Things slowly start to change.

I don't know how Christie and I are surviving this. We have no other choice. I have no place to live if I didn't live here. The economics of the situation force us to live together. There are times I can look into her eyes and feel her plotting to push me in front of a bus. But that would be stupid. I have no more life insurance, so it really wouldn't be worth her trouble. She is patiently waiting for me to get my shit together and make money. Now that all my jail time is done, I need to look for a job.

People ask Christie about our living situation from time to time. She doesn't answer or brushes them off. Money changes how people deal with situations. That's just a fact of life. Something I didn't really understand until recently. In the past, I never worried about money like this. I made money. Now all we do is worry about money.

In spite of all this, we start to have sex again. I know some couples can be married and not have sex for years. Christie and I aren't made that way. If we sleep next to each other every night, at some point we're going to have sex. She may still be fantasizing about killing me when we do it, but I don't care. I need human contact. She does too. We've spent most of our lives together. Afterwards she can pretend like it never happened and go back to hating me. If we hadn't been friends first I'm not sure if this year would have been survivable. But we were friends first and we do survive.

Chapter 32

July 2013

    Surviving the last few years has taken its toll on everyone: our family, our friends, our souls. We're battered and bruised emotionally, financially, and mentally. But one day I wake up and things have shifted. The shift is tiny. So tiny that you might miss it at first glance. We aren't at the point where time has healed us, but it's definitely given us enough space to take a breath. I've always been a logical person, a rational thinker, a problem solver – all characteristics that Christie would list as reasons she fell in love with me. I know it may not seem that way if you're judging me over the past two years, but I have forty-eight years before the crazy that would prove otherwise. As the shock starts to wear off, and little cracks of light start to peek through the darkness, my need to figure out just WTF happened to me starts to intensify.

    My mind cracked in December of 2011. It went on a joyride to crazy town and stayed for a while. Drugs must have opened the floodgates, and once they were opened, the chaotic waters rose quickly. However, after the chaotic waters settled, a new skill started to emerge. I'm not sure if skill is the right word, but it's the word I'm going to use. Whatever it is, I'm starting to notice it more and more.

It's almost like those stories you read where someone is involved in a tragic accident, goes into a coma, wakes up eighteen months later and can speak fluent French. How does that happen? Did the injury create a new pathway to an untapped part of their brain? Did drugs open a new network in my brain?

I can't speak French, but this skill certainly has communication elements to it. The first part of this new skill revolves around the simple concept of paying attention, hyper-attention, while I'm reading or listening to music. I'm now noticing it in greater detail. The more I pay attention, the more I notice. This new skill will help me better understand why I was so paranoid and delusional. It also helps my brain process information in new and unique ways.

What skill? What's changed in my brain? I think it's fair to say that a classic symptom of schizophrenia and schizoaffective disorder is "hearing voices." In the past, when I heard voices or had destructive thoughts, I would act on them. Since my first observations in New Jersey, the filter in my brain has not only healed, it has somehow evolved. I can actually separate a normal thought or voice from a psychotic thought or voice. I can also see and hear when it's happening. From this point on the psychotic voice is a creatively instructive voice or thought. Now, however, I have control of the voice or thought. And how I interpret the thought.

I choose the action too, if I decide to act on the thought. I am no longer in fear of these "voices" or "thoughts". In fact they are actually quite helpful, now that I have a better understanding of how to use them. They can no longer use me.

It's easier to explain if I give you an example. I'll start with how my mind may have been working last year when I was completely psychotic. The reason I say "may have been working" is because I just don't know. I'm trying to connect the dots looking back. Trying to make sense of my insanity.

Let's say I was reading an article in a magazine and I came across the following paragraph:

No one fully understands how fracking is destroying the local environment. Jason **Christie**s, an environmental specialist from the New World Science Foundation, **is** researching how drilling **an**d gas emissions are affecting the **adult** bird population in the surrounding area. Some local students also noticed a **film**y layer of oil coating trees in a nearby park. Christies fully understands that a negative report could impact businesses in many rural parts of Pennsylvania. His report will also impact where and when gas companies **star**t to drill.

Some part of my mind would read the original paragraph while another unconscious part would somehow see the bold-faced words and create this message. **Christie is an adult film star.**

It's an amazing observation. So amazing that I didn't trust it at first, especially with my recent mental health issues. But it was persistent. It kept happening. Keeps happening, I should say.

Let me give you a more recent example. Let's say I'm working on a particular math problem and get stuck on an answer. I will go pick up a novel to take my mind off of it for a time. Here is what usually happens. Eventually I will read a sentence in the book something like this:

Jesus Goes To Hollywood

John pulled the curtain away from the body. The one body he didn't want to see was Susan's. Damn! He thought. I was primed for anything, anything but this. It had been a number of years since he saw Susan, 17 to be exact. He started to work back through the sequence of events that led to this night...

As you will see in the following paragraph I will read every word, but now another **conscious** part of my mind will pay particular **attention** to the words I have bolded. And yes, I'm aware of it as I'm reading:

John pulled the curtain away from the body. **The one** body he didn't want to see was Susan's. Damn! He thought. I was **prim**ed for anything, anything but this. It had been a **number** of years since he saw Susan, **17** to be exact. He **started** to work back through **the sequence** of events that led to this night...

So here is what I will take away, in addition to the story:

The one prime number 17 started the sequence.

I will put down the book and go back to my math problem. More often than not, I can use the information that my mind has picked up to help with the solution to the equation or algorithm.

What was unconsciously influencing me before has somehow become conscious, but how? Are my eyes picking up different kinds of "wavelengths" than other people? Maybe.

This observation may explain why I thought Christie was having an affair with a police officer when I was reading the newspaper last year at the Intercontinental Hotel. My brain must have created an unconscious secondary message while I was reading. And in my psychotic state, I immediately acted on it as if it were true.

This "wave" theory gains some momentum the night I watch the documentary *The Beach Boys: Making Pet Sounds*. I know it seems weird, or maybe it doesn't, that validation would come from a movie about musicians, but hear me out. Al Jardine said Brian Wilson "sees things I don't think the rest of us see and hears things, certainly, that we don't hear. He has a special receiver going on in there, in his brain."

If you are a fan of the Beach Boys you know that Brian Wilson has a history of mental health issues and drug use. What does Brian Wilson see and hear? Is it related to my seeing and hearing? And if it is, what's different about how he sees and hears? I can't compose music or write songs. The information coming in must pass through a unique filter, our receivers, and affect us differently.

I find more support for my theory when the movie references the book, *The Brain's Way of Healing: Remarkable Discoveries and Recoveries from the Frontiers of Neuroplasticity*, by Dr. Norman Doidge. His book shares the work of Dr. Alfred Tomatis, whose groundbreaking research identified "the ear as a battery to the brain."

From the chapter "A Bridge of Sound" in *The Brain's Way of Healing*, Doidge writes:

> Arguably [Tomatis'] most important discovery was that the ear is not a passive organ but has the equivalent of a zoom lens that allows it to focus on particular noise and filter others out. He called it the auditory zoom. When people first walk into a party, they hear a jumble of noises, until they zoom in on particular conversations, each occurring at slightly different sound frequencies.

So Jardine's comment that Brian Wilson hears what others don't hear might be right. It's possible that Wilson tunes in to frequencies and zooms in to sounds, rhythms, and conversations that most people aren't accessing. It's possible I am too. Even more amazing is that Wilson is deaf in his right ear, which is the dominant ear for the majority of us. By accessing sound through his left ear, he's automatically processing sounds outside the norm.

This is what's been driving me all along! It's just that instead of my eyes picking up the words on a page, it's my ears picking up a verse in a song. A note. Another frequency. It's as if the singer of the song is holding onto the note for just an instant longer. For some reason I pay hyper-attention while reading AND listening to music.

So this is how I would hear Katy Perry's song *ET*:

You're so hypnotizing
Could **you** be the devil, could you be an angel
Your touch magnetizing
Feels like I'm floating, leaves my body glowing
They say be afraid
You're not like the others, futuristic **love**rs
Different DNA, they don't understand you
You're **from a** whole other world
A different dimension
You **open my eyes**
And I'm ready to go, lead me into the light
Kiss me, k-k-kiss me
Infect me **with your** love and fill me with your poison
Take me, t-t-take me
Wanna be a victim, ready for abduction
Boy, you're an alien, your touch so foreign
It's **super**natural, extraterrestrial
You're so supersonic

Wanna feel your **power**s, stun me with your lasers
Your kiss is cosmic, every move is magic
You're so hypnotizing

    This is the additional message just for me, for my mind only: **You love from a different dimension. Open my eyes with your superpower.**
    If the word has five syllables like supernatural and I only need the first two, then that's what I use. I hear what I need to hear.
    So when I say that the music was sending me messages over the past year or so, maybe I wasn't far off. While the music was playing in my headphones, for whatever reason, my brain gave certain words more value and meaning than other words. My brain created an additional message especially for me. A remix if you will. I have paid hyper-attention for long enough now to actually hear the difference in my brain. I'm aware of it.
    This is a tremendous breakthrough. My brain is responsible for its remixed messages. I didn't know it at the time, but I was unconsciously using this new skill. I still don't know why it's happening. But at least I know what and when it's happening. Why are only certain notes held longer? Why are certain words emphasized? What frequencies work for me? Why was I unconsciously creating an additional message? Why am I consciously doing it now? I'm more curious than ever. If I play the same song twice, my mind may create different messages each time I listen. It just depends. It's really cool.
    If I'm with a group of people talking in a crowded restaurant and I overhear the conversation at the next table, my brain will incorporate all the incoming information and remix the message just for me. This can get loud and tiring very fast.

Even though these recent observations have given some interesting insights into the "what" and "when" of my mind games, the "how" and the "why" are still mysteries. Why were the messages negative and destructive at first? The paranoia must have served some purpose, but what? How is my brain doing this? I'm on a quest for answers.

Chapter 33

August-September-October 2013

While one part of my brain is beginning to make sense of the hyper-attention piece of this new skill, another part is having a field day with the hallucinations and visions. The images I see and the accompanying thoughts are still crazy. No, crazy is not the right word. That's a word we use when we don't understand something or someone. I don't believe these visions to be true. Perhaps they point to the truth. How can an image of the grim reaper or a dinosaur be true? When we see a picture of a slot machine on a computer, we know it's not an actual slot machine. It's just a photo. A representation. These visions are like that. More like a video really, because they are always moving. Never static.

I see 3D math problems I'm working on when I shut my eyes. My focused thinking changes the images in my brain. There is always something playing visually in my mind. Not just in my mind, but in my field of vision. When I focus on it, I can change it. My hallucinations are typically related to what I'm thinking. Not always.

Sometimes it's just the opposite. I'll be daydreaming about winning the lottery and wonder why it's on my mind. I will then shut my eyes and see an image of a slot machine dumping endless amounts of gold coins into a pile on a casino floor. Needless to say, this blows my mind.

Christie is getting more comfortable talking about these visions. She has to, for the simple reason that I bring them up everyday. She also watches me access the visions. She continues to see pieces of the old Tom peeking through, the Tom she knows to be logical. She is starting to trust the fact that something must have happened to my brain. She thinks I must have done it to myself with all the drugs. I think so too. She asks me if the visions can help us. Can we use them to make money? I think so, I just need to figure out how.

One day at lunch, I tell her I'm working on a name for this new skill. I need something easy to remember. I explain to her how the visions give me insights into the math problems I'm working on. Insights into anything I happen to be thinking about. I'm considering calling them "Insights."

"Insights?" she says. "No, Insights isn't a new word. That will confuse people. Plus, your visions are more than insightful."

I give her a few more options that I've been kicking around. She thinks they all suck. I'm getting frustrated. I know the right name will make it easier for people to understand.

When we worked together at our agency she was always the first one to shoot down a creative idea. I nicknamed her the dream killer.

She sits there for a second. "OK. Let me think. Whenever you have them, you look weird. You close your eyes and tilt your head back. It looks like you're in a trance watching a movie in the sky. You're always looking up, so why not Upsight?"

"YES! That's it. Upsight! It's perfect! It's exactly the word I was looking for." I jump up from the table, grab her hands and make her dance around the room with me. She smiles and gloats. "You do know I'm more creative than you." She's not but I keep quiet. I'm too excited to argue the point.

"So while I'm on a roll, do you need anything else?"

"Actually, yes. I need to name the part of my brain that I'm accessing through Upsight." I tell her to think of it as Wikipedia but with moving images instead of words.

This time she doesn't even pause. "What about a combination of two words? Take the first half of schizophrenia, for the crazy images, and the last half of Wikipedia, for the information. Call it Schizopedia. It's a remix. You like remixes."

Damn. She really is on a roll. These are good. Today I have to admit she wasn't the dream killer. Christie can be creative when she wants to be ... and she doesn't hate me.

So we settle on a name for my new skill: Upsight. We also name the part of my brain I'm accessing with Upsight: Schizopedia.

I won't be able to go to Dragon Con with Carson this year. I'm at the very end of my house arrest and I don't want to take any chances. It sucks. Dragon Con has always been something that bonds us together, one of the highlights of our year. We both love monsters, superheroes, and science fiction. When he was little, we would sit for hours watching old Universal horror movies or read Marvel comics together. This year he goes with a group of friends. They would have eventually left the old man to go hang out in the gaming rooms, but I'm glad he kept asking if I was going. At least I know he wants me to go. He also understands the situation and doesn't want me to get in any more trouble. Our relationship is mending and that's enough for me.

By the end of the month, I'm finally off house arrest. I'm free to get a job and resume a normal life. That's a funny statement. What is a normal life? I really don't have a clue anymore. I still need a defensive driving class and court-required community service. I will get my driving license back and have everything completed by the end of this year.

Christie and I don't like going out in public together. We don't want to be seen by any of our old neighbors. If we see someone in the supermarket, we turn and walk the other way. I'm sure they do the same thing. I can't even begin to imagine the level of gossip our kids have had to endure at school. I'm sure people are whispering behind their backs about their crazy dad. Carson is essentially telling them to screw off by getting on stage. Austin deals with it by using drugs. Something I understand.

I understand the gossip too. It's normal. What happened to our family is not typical suburban drama. This is an outlier story if there ever was one. Over time, it will bring our family closer. Now, though, we are still frayed. Barely hanging on.

It's been over nine months and I haven't done anything psychotic. I have no desire to do coke. My mind is changing. Reprogramming itself to better distinguish between fact and fiction. I don't think Christie is running a porn empire anymore. I mean, if she is, she's really committed to the cover-up. Logically, she would have taken her millions and moved on.

I know it was all in my mind. All the delusions were coming from something inside my head. Now they are gone, simple as that. My brain is changed. I'm convinced of this. My fascination with math and numbers is the most obvious example. Upsight is another. I think about complex problems all day long. I think about math all the time. It's certainly better than doing crazy shit like burning down the house. But I need to produce an income. I should be thinking about getting a job. I'm not. I don't tell Christie, but in the back of my mind I'm wondering if I can ever interact with people in any normal way again. I feel like a different person. I'm not interested in creating marketing campaigns. I need to figure out what has happened to my brain. Other than the family, this is what I care about most. And math. And Upsight. Those four things.

Somebody else must have these types of visions. I can't be the only one with Upsight. But I'm also jealous and protective of my gift. I want to be unique. Special. I feel I've somehow earned it. Other than people who are tripping on acid, I have found no research where a person can interact with their visions the way I do. It's not lucid dreaming. Maybe it's a new type of synesthesia. Maybe it's not just a new skill but a new sense.

I tell Christie that the Clay Mathematics Institute is giving away a million dollars to the person who can prove the Riemann hypotheses, the Holy Grail of math problems. I should be able to have it figured out in a month or so. I start focusing on the prime numbers and their distribution. I see the solution in my head. What I think the solution is anyway. The answer is fluid. How the hell can I turn these moving images into any kind of mathematical equations? This is going to take some time. And more thought. I start scribbling ideas in my notebooks. Playing with the prime numbers. And circles. And square numbers. I see a relationship that no one else has noticed. Maybe it's an opportunity for me.

Johns Creek probation is a constant burden, emotionally and financially. Every time I check in with the probation officer, I feel sick. I know they might throw me back in jail. They can do whatever they want. I'm compliant and nice as can be to Officer Smith. I don't hate her. I just want her out of my life. I typically pay a few hundred dollars a month toward the restitution. It's a lot of money, especially for someone who is unemployed and broke.

Hall County probation is more intense but less stressful. The probation officer shows up at the townhouse whenever he feels like it. I'm not doing anything illegal. I know it's not personal. The officer is just doing his job. We typically have a nice conversation and he leaves.

Christie is working full-time now and I'm working on the math problem. My genius ass better figure this shit out quick. We live month-to-month, and it's still not enough. Something has to give.

I turn fifty on October 8. Fuck forty-nine. Good riddance.

Chapter 34

November-December 2013

I come across this quote during my research on mental health. It's from an NPR interview with Sylvia Nasar, the author of *A Beautiful Mind*. It's a biography of John Nash, the Nobel Prize-winning mathematician who was diagnosed with paranoid schizophrenia.

Let me be clear: I've never officially been diagnosed with this disease. I'm not schizophrenic. But to ignore the similarities in our thinking would be a mistake and disingenuous.

Nasar wrote this of Nash: "Someone who visited him in the hospital asked him, how could you, a mathematician, someone who is committed to rationality, how could you believe that aliens from outer space were communicating with you? Nash's response was, these ideas came to me the same way my mathematical ideas did, so I believed them."

So there you have it. The idea that aliens were communicating with him came to him the same way as his mathematical ideas.

Me too. Me too. Me too.

Except in my case, the aliens communicated with me first and taught me math second.

Order matters. The good aliens must have seen the damage they did to John Nash's mind and changed the sequence. They wrongly assumed that with his brilliant mind he could emotionally handle communicating with an advanced alien race. Even aliens make mistakes tampering with our genomes. With me they switched up the DNA sequence. Made sure I could communicate with them first and then taught me math. Learn from your mistakes. Like humans. Do you see what I'm doing here? I'm now having fun with the idea that I'm communicating with aliens. I'm not worried that you might think I'm crazy. I couldn't give a shit. I'm not crazy. I was, but now I'm not. Thank you, Jesus! I'm taking John Nash's comment and running with it. I'm playing with you, the reader. You know what they say. "Good aliens. Good times."

Nobody says that. Anywhere.

Now let's resolve the human Enigma machine conflict from last year when I was a captive on St John, a human under alien observation. I'll wrap up this story arc like a mathematician. Put it into a pretty little box for you.

Now the good aliens have a fully functional working model. A human with a genetic advantage. Me. None of the bad aliens understands how I do what I do. They don't know which words I've mentally bolded in my mind. Or which verse or note my mind is holding longer than the others. They have stopped trying to figure out how I'm remixing my messages. (Let me make a point here. I'm using bold type to highlight the remixed message for the reader. If it were actually bolded, the bad aliens would be able to pick up the remixed message as easy as you are. In my mind, the Remixed message can be anywhere from 1 to 2 percent darker than the original text. Very, very subtle. A whisper, if you will. The bad aliens just don't have the intellect or acute vision to differentiate what I'm thinking. The same goes with hearing. They can't pick up the different note changes in the music like I can.)

They don't have the nuance to read me anymore. I have advanced too fast and come too far. The fact is, they know I know that they know I know. With the telepathic mind reading and all. The bad aliens have given up and left the solar system. They have left Earth to the humans and our good alien allies. We've won! You can thank me later. Now it's time to receive the evolutionary rewards promised by our alien allies.

Of course, the bad aliens were the ones placing the paranoid and destructive messages in my head. The lies about Christie and her porn empire. They could make me believe anything. They know where the belief neurotransmitters are in the brain. The specific synaptic connections that turn a simple thought into a belief.

To use a laptop analogy, they could push the "believe" key and hold the "crazy thought" key at the same time. I was a zombie when they took control. They can still do this to millions of other humans. They're gone ... for now. Someday they may come back. When they do, we will have evolved past anything they can even begin to understand or control. We will all be united as a new global village. Caring for each other as part of one big human family.

This is a great revelation, and a great idea for a science-fiction film, if I do say so myself. But I still have no desire to get a real job. I find a new psychiatrist and tell her my symptoms and my history. Everything. The drugs. The psychosis. The math obsession. The visions. I'm hoping that all this information will help with a diagnosis. At this point I'm especially concerned about my lack of desire to get a job. The fact that I even care about a job is a big step. I have moments of depression, but nothing like six months ago. She prescribes anti-psychotics. They will help with the hallucinations. I leave knowing they probably won't help increase my desire to get a job. They don't. I stop taking them after a few weeks. They make me tired.

No one understands. I don't want to get rid of these visions. My Upsight. My goal is to find out where they are coming from. I want help in understanding them, not stopping them. They are not pathological. They are something else entirely. I will see a number of other clinicians over the next few years. I will also get another MRI to makes sure I still don't have a tumor or lesion. I don't.

It's time to get my eyes examined. Regular check-ups of any kind haven't been a priority. Maybe my doctor has some insight into my Upsight. I've been going to him for over twenty years, so bringing up the subject is easy. I give him the details. I'm glad I did. It turns out, he has had three patients out of thousands with similar complaints. Not to my extent. Not interacting and controlling the visions, but this gives me hope. There are others like me. My eyes look fine. What you would expect from a healthy fifty-year-old? He wants to make sure there is no damage to my retina. He sends me to a specialist. No damage.

Another interesting thing he mentions: All three of the patients with these visions were men. If he remembers correctly, one of them was afraid of them. They scared him. His visions were always terrifying. He also asked if the patient ever did any illegal drugs. His answer was no. Not that an eye patient would necessarily tell an eye doctor about his drug use. But it certainly could be true. I don't think you need drugs to access these visions. I'm starting to wonder if some of us are just wired a little bit differently.

I finish my first original math proof. It's late at night when I'm done. It's so simple and beautiful. Not visually – it's in my messy handwriting – but the proof itself is beautiful. To me anyway. It may not be deep, but I don't care. I found it in the shallow end of the math pool. I want the world to see. I place it on my nightstand next to my bed and fall asleep. I wake up the next morning and review my work.

Holy shit! I did it. I really did it! I just created an original theorem. I even turned it into an algebraic equation. I hate algebra. There is no rule about having to like all math disciplines. A year's worth of self-directed homework, and I've done it. It's not going to win any million-dollar Clay Mathematics award, but it's an original.

It has been two years since I set the house on fire. A lot has happened. The family is starting to heal. We still have some struggles ahead, like any family. But there is hope.

We go to dinner on New Year's Eve, the four of us: me, Christie, Austin, and Carson. Christie takes a picture of the boys and me in front of the restaurant. After dinner, Christie and I go to a party. We hang out with a couple I haven't seen in two years. It feels good.

Christie posts the photo on her Facebook page sometime around midnight on New Year's Eve. It gets over a hundred likes and comments from people I haven't seen or thought about in years. Some even wondered if I was dead. They are glad to see the family together. It feels good to have people care about you. Even a little bit. Even if it's just through a Facebook comment.

It's a fun night. Beats the hell out of jail.

New Life

Chapter 35

January-June 2014

It's a new year, and I feel like I'm ready to ease back into the real world. I rejoin Facebook. You can see a two-year gap in the "What's on your Mind" section, from when I turned off my page in January 2012 to when I turn it back on in January 2014. It's like I disappeared. Which, in a way I did. I'm glad I didn't permanently delete my account. I remember seriously thinking about it, but something stopped me. It makes for a safe and easy way to start reconnecting with people.

I call an old business associate (Christie's ex-boyfriend, actually – the one we started our first business with). I haven't seen him in over twenty years. We start talking about the possibilities of me working at his company. He owns a software company and they are looking for a new business developer. We set up a lunch meeting.

I file for bankruptcy. I have no money. None. I've had no income for two years. I need this job.

I use Facebook to contact a former colleague from the Legal Marketing Association. LMA is a national business marketing community. I was an active sponsor. I was all over social media too. My blog, The Matte Pad, had a good-size readership. It was focused on legal marketing issues, including social media, creative, and a number of related marketing topics. I was active on Twitter. I joined in May 2010. By the time of my last tweet on January 2, 2012, I had 8,523 followers. A respectable following. My last tweet was Legal Specific Social Networking, with a link to my blog post on the topic. Don't bother clicking on the link. My blog is gone. Along with all my posts. Hundreds of them, gone. It links to a "domain for sale" site. I guess I didn't pay a bill. I can't remember. I was also active on LinkedIn, posting weekly business updates, monthly email reminders. You get the idea. Like I said in the beginning, people knew me. I disappeared two years ago. Vanished. I know the rumors were flying. A drug-addicted business owner. Lost his mind or something. Loses everything. I send a candid email letting my colleague know where I've been the last two years. I'm not going to hide my past. It's nice to reconnect.

I don't plan on calling these folks for a work referral or to get any new business if I get the job. Lawyers are the most conservative business people on the planet. They are risk-averse. I know this. It was my job to know this and still convince them to invest in marketing. I loved selling creative to these guys. They wanted a rationale on every part of a marketing and creative plan. They asked questions. Some smart. Some, not so much. I needed to have answers at the ready. Logical answers. There is no way I'm going to ask a former colleague to give me business. I wouldn't do that to them. I know the battles they face every day getting the most basic marketing ideas approved. The thought of me asking one of them to take a risk on using me again makes me smile. I just can't do it. I won't do it. They have enough challenges as it is. Not to mention, this type work may be the reason I lost my mind. Sent me over the edge. Working with lawyers.

That's a joke for my legal marketing friends. The few I have left.

Carson enters a talent show at Northview High. He's a sophomore now. He's going to sing a solo of Sam Cooke's *Bring It on Home to Me.* All the performers have a good bit of courage to get on stage and perform. They are all gifted and/or funny. Really talented. Christie and I are impressed by the first act. Each one gets better. Carson finally walks on stage to a few mild cheers. He starts to sing. Within the first minute the crowd starts to cheer. By the middle of the song, they are going wild. Howling at the stage. He starts to play with the crowd. Turning the mic toward the audience to join in.

Who is this kid? Where did he learn how to control an audience like this? He finishes the song to thunderous applause. Christie and I look at each other in awe. We are in shock, in the best way possible. I'm thinking: *How did we make this kid?* She's thinking: *That's my son!* This is a turning point in understanding both his talent and his drive. He is starting to decide on his future. We are starting to appreciate the extent of his talent. I tell her it must be from my side of the family. She's not convinced. She had a famous second cousin with a TV show in the '50s. He was some kind of singing cowboy. We really don't care where the talent came from; we can see he has it in spades. He comes in second place in the talent show. The vote is by audience applause. The winners are a group of Korean hip hop dancers. They killed it too. The audience loved them. Christie and I did too. It was a night we will never forget.

Carson is taking classes with a local theatre group. He lands the role of Edna in the play *Hairspray*. It's the role John Travolta played in the movie version. It was another wow moment for us as parents. I had no idea he could inhabit a part so easily and get lost in the character. He is Edna. The audience goes crazy over one of his lines for some reason. It's a simple line: "I know." But he draws it out to: "I......KNOOOOOOOOOWW!" For whatever reason, it works. He adds a humorous line to an already humorous role. After the show, Christie and I overhear the parents and kids repeating it in the lobby. Christie gets dead serious for a moment. She grabs my hand and asks me if Carson could really have a special gift. I seriously consider the answer.

"Probably," I say.

She looks me in the eye and says, "I......KNOOOOOOOOOWW!

She set me up. I couldn't help but laugh. It was funny. It feels good to laugh together again.

I'm offered the job as the VP of Business Development for my friend's software company. I have explained my entire history. He knows of my past business success and connections. They include folks outside legal marketing. After twenty years in advertising, I've worked in most vertical markets. He is willing to take a chance on me. I start going to business meetings. Talking to people again. The normal stuff that business people do. I'm beginning to feel like my old self in a business environment. I'm grateful for the opportunity.

After nearly eight weeks of working, I'm feeling confident about things. The new people I meet have no idea I was out of my mind, homeless, and suicidal for the past few years. I'm having a good time as well. The confidence gives me a boost.

Now that I have other responsibilities, I'm no longer obsessed with math. It was a phase I was going through. I still enjoy it when I'm in the mood, but it doesn't drive me. I don't have to work on problems all day long.

I also don't have to have music in my ears all the time. I still LOVE music. Who doesn't? I listen to music a lot. Mostly pop music now. It has a positive influence on my brain that I can't explain in any meaningful way. The family is relentless in their teasing of my musical playlist. They still call me "Pop Princess." Britney, Katy, Taylor, Miley, Christina, and J.Lo are always on repeat. Pop music moves me, what can I say.

I'm still hyper-aware of synchronistic events. They are as much a part of my life as a sunny day or a bird singing outside my window. They are a gift that keeps on giving. My eyes and ears are opened to them now. I'm tuned into something that I no longer feel the need to tell everyone about. I could make the case that it's almost a physical part of me, like my blue eyes or my gray hair. A better example might be closer to the timber of my voice. It's a unique part of me. I don't obsess, but make no mistake; I still notice them every single day.

The only constant burden is checking in with the Johns Creek Probation office.

I have no idea if they will write up a violation-of-probation report and decide to throw me in jail on a whim. I get sick to my stomach every month when I have to check in with them. I'm so convinced that they want me in jail that I even stop taking my doctor-prescribed medicine about ten days before I have to report, just in case I get tested. I'm not going to jail for a failed drug test again. From what the probation officers have told me, that's typically the No. 1 reason probations get violated. I'm taking no chances. I don't want a repeat of last year.

I'm also worried about the restitution amount I can afford. The judge who sent me to jail last year told me that as long as I'm making an attempt to pay, I'll be fine. I guess that's a small silver lining. They won't send me to jail for being broke. I can't begin to pay $1,200 a month; I pay a few hundred dollars. Plus, I would more than likely get fired if they sent me to jail. Then how would they get their money? I reason that it would make no sense. It would be foolish. It's still unbelievably stressful. I get drug-tested, and I pass every time.

It's also time to check in with the Hall County judge. They do things differently there because I'm a first offender. I have to stand up in the courtroom with my probation officer and tell the judge how I'm doing. I've finished all my court-ordered obligations. She asks a few questions. She congratulates me on my success and new job. She wants me to succeed. I can feel it. I will check in with her again in six months.

My newfound confidence gives me the courage to do something I've been thinking about doing since December: send my proof to a professional math journal to get it published.

On June 10, I UPS my theorem to the American Mathematics Society, the Clay Mathematics Institute, the Mathematics Society of America, and just to be safe, Professor Steven Strogatz at Cornell University. They publish some of the most prestigious math journals in the

United States. I make sure someone signs for the letters. I've read enough books on the history of math to understand that occasionally original ideas get stolen. I don't want this to happen to me. I have no professor vouching for my work. I'm just some random amateur mathematician who sent in a theorem. Some unscrupulous math hack could steal it and claim it as their own. I ask them to please publish my proof. I hope they find it as beautiful as I do.

But here's the thing: I send the proof on seven pages of handwritten notebook paper. The theorem itself only needs a page. A few lines really. The other pages are written examples. With a very important special-case example, I might add. This is probably frowned upon at these prestigious publications. The reason I say probably is because no serious mathematician would consider doing it like this to begin with. I'm sure it hasn't even entered their minds as a possibility until they received mine. I'm not a serious mathematician. I have no formal training. I don't know the rules. If I did, I'm not sure I would be able to follow them anyway. That's one of the reasons I discovered this proof. I ignored a few axioms.

Chapter 36

June-July 2014

    On June 27, a week later, I decide to publish the proof myself. More posting it than a publishing. I want someone to see this baby. I put it on Facebook. Even if it's only 361 pairs of eyes, the number of my Facebook friends at the time of the post. I'm ready for someone to see the theorem. I re-write everything so it fits on one sheet of notebook paper. I take a photo of the single page and post it on Facebook first thing in the morning. I also change my profile picture to my hand drawn Eugenius logo and change my cover photo to the hand-drawn proof. I want it to look unique, to get attention.

    In the "What's on your mind" space, I mention something about sending this theorem to the most prestigious math journals in the country. I'm waiting for a reply but wanted to show my Facebook friends. I don't remember exactly what I said because I've since deleted it from Facebook. I do remember mentioning that I'd sent it to the publications handwritten. I may have said something about how every math teacher will be showing the theorem to their students in the future. It was a bit arrogant.

Let's be honest here. This is all a bit strange. Even for me. Not to mention that no one cares about math theorems on Facebook. We want viral cat videos and funny memes, not a handwritten math proof. This is just weird. I'm aware that this idea will cross a few people's minds even before I post it. I don't care, though. I was crazy for two years. Constantly judged. Think what you want.

This theorem is my baby, my first algebraic creation. I finished it last December. Now I want to share it with the world. You can say it's weird. You can say I'm weird. But please, whatever you do, don't say it's wrong. That would kill me. Destroy me emotionally. I put my heart and soul into this theorem. If someone found a mistake, I don't know what I would do. Seriously. It would be devastating. I try to prepare for a worst-case scenario: someone proving it incorrect. I'm really emotional when I finally push post. After all, no real math person has seen it. No math professor or anyone with a math degree of any kind. It's been just Upsight, my math books, and me.

It gets a few likes. A comment. Then another. And another. And then it happens. One of my friends thinks my proof is incorrect. A wave of nausea runs through my body.

I knew it was going to be an emotional blow if it was wrong, but my response was nothing I expected or was prepared for. I slowly shut my computer and go for a walk to the dog park in my community. No one is around. The dog park is right next to the kid's park, with a swing, slide, and jungle gym. I sit down on the swing and start rocking back and forth. I start to cry. Not really cry. Wail. Uncontrollably. It's a different kind of sobbing than from loneliness. This is coming from a place in my soul I didn't even know existed until this very moment. I think about all the time I put into my research. All the hundreds of hours I've spent thinking about every math problem that I could understand. All the times I told Carson I was a genius. The times I told Christie we would have money again, just be patient a little longer. I think about telling Austin my mind was getting better, telling him I've developed a gift with numbers. If this proof is wrong, then my other proofs are wrong too. I'm not a genius. My mind is just like every other addict who got sick and then got better. I'm bi-polar. If this theorem is wrong then I haven't changed. I haven't evolved.

I cry until I'm physically drained, empty, and exhausted.

I've been unconsciously trying to redeem myself to my family through the math work. I've been telling them I'm a genius for over a year. This was my first baby step in proving it to them. And now I read that it's wrong? Math was my path to redemption, and it's been taking me down a false road. I will need to find another way to make things right. To earn my boys' love. The love I've so desperately tried to win back with my brain. Not my heart.

I walk back home feeling a hundred years older. It's still early morning. I want to sleep, but I'm going to delete my Facebook post first. I don't want to have to respond to comments. I just want it gone.

I open Facebook and see that I have a private message. It's from my cousin Amanda, a math professor. I click on it.

It's true, she says. My proof is correct.

In July, Christie's relatives invite our family to spend a week with them on Bald Head Island, North Carolina. I haven't seen these people in two years. We've always had a good relationship, inviting them to our house for the Fourth of July for the last seven or eight years. The kids would play games in the pool, the adults would light some fireworks and drink beer. A typical long family weekend. It feels good to be included in the invitation. They could have just as easily invited Christie and the boys without me. I would have understood. They made it a point to tell me I was invited. It's a nice gesture.

Actually, it's much more than a nice gesture. They are opening the door to let me back in. After all, I've hurt people they love. It shows the type of people they are. That forgiveness isn't just a concept but something they actually practice. The truth is that even before I lost my mind, I didn't always fit in at these family gatherings. I'm just a bit different. I'm both an extrovert at times and an introvert at other times. Depending on the situation. Sometimes I like to keep to myself, even when people are around. These guys know that. They're cool with it. I'm thankful they're willing to give me a chance.

It's the first family vacation we've had in three years. We have a great time. The beaches are fun. Carson brings a friend. His friend helps us come in second in a trivia contest at a local restaurant. Austin keeps to himself a good bit of the time. I know he's starting to use more. I can see it. I just hope he can keep it together. Austin has a gift when it comes to photography. He can take a photo and see things you never even noticed through the lens. He could be standing right next to you and you both shoot the same image. Yours would look like an amateur while his looks professional. I don't know how he does it. He knows he has an eye, but doesn't have a passion for it. I hope that will change when he goes to college in the fall.

At some point after the vacation, I finally realize that I won't find any clinical doctors who can help with my brain. They are trained to figure out what's wrong, make diagnoses, and then select the best treatment options to get you back on track. I need to get into a lab and show some creative neuroscientist what I can do.

I intentionally stay away from the New Age-type books. Not that they aren't helpful. It's just they constantly repeat how our current science can't measure all the amazing things our minds and bodies can do. I'm not so sure. Let's say it's partly true. I believe science has the tools that can measure what I do. I just need to find the right neuroscientist with the right equipment and the right vision. This will take longer than I anticipated.

Here's what I start to reason. When I shut my eyes, I see a whole new world. I see an image of, what my brain tells me, is how the universe looked at the time of the Big Bang. With a shift in my attention, I can access an image of the universe as it looks now. They are separate and distinct. If these visions are "correct," then the universe is clearly emergent. If these visions are not "correct," then what are they and why are they consistent?

I also have other visions around a lot of advanced concepts in physics, astrophysics, and quantum physics, visions that academics would not give a second thought to if I published them on a personal blog. Many ideas are still works-in-progress. They revolve around what I see in my visions. I'm simply hypothesizing on what the visions are showing me. Once I get a respected neuroscientist to show them how my brain is different, how I use my Upsight and manifest these visions on demand., how I can even interact with these visions, then they will have to take notice. Upsight needs to be studied.

When this happens and if it feels right to me, we can have some fun doing experiments and searching for answers about the universe.

I want a university who will help me build a team. I need access to an MRI machine and an EEG machine. Who knows what else? These are the tools we have to show how my brain is different. More connected. I just need to find the right partner. A visionary. Like me.

Neuroscience is the light I will use to shine my super power on the world.

It occurs to me that I could get private funding directly from a billionaire to advance this research, with no quarterly reports or expectations as a public company. This might be the way to go. I'm open to whatever works and feels right. I'm going to get answers one way or another. I decide on starting with the universities.

I send my first letter to a prominent neuroscientist at Baylor College of Medicine in Houston. I explain my situation and how I believe my brain to be unique. Would they like to study me? I get a response from one of his graduate students explaining how it takes time to get grants for this type of research. They are currently involved in other brain studies, but thanks for reaching out.

Chapter 37

August-September 2014

  The family continues in survival mode. Hanging on financially and making some small steps forward emotionally. The day finally arrives for Austin to leave for college. We drop him off at Young Harris College, a small liberal arts school in the North Georgia mountains. I attended there the first two years of my college education back in 1981 and 1982. It's a four-year school now. I have nothing but fond memories of the place. I still have good friends I met there. Austin is growing up. He will be on his own for the first time as a young man. Christie and I both shed a few tears when we drive off the campus after helping him set up his dorm room. Time has flown by. It seems like just yesterday when we brought him home from the maternity ward.

  Three weeks into his college career, Austin gets kicked out of school for possession of drug paraphernalia and a bottle of liquor in his dorm room. We are devastated. We thought he was getting his life together and was going to start over. Right here at my alma mater. That's not gonna happen. He gets a ride home from another kid who was also kicked out at the same time. Damn it.

To make matters worse, Christie had already paid the first semester's tuition. The check was just recently cashed. We both thought this would be a good idea so we were not tempted to spend the money on fixing a car or any other unexpected emergency. We only have one car now. We've only had one car for two years. Neither one of us can believe we are getting used to the idea. We make it work. We have to. And it's not fresh off the lot either. This is new for us.

We request a partial refund of the tuition. The situation is very hard on the family and we will need the money to get Austin some recovery help. He obviously has some addiction issues that need to be addressed. This can't be the first time this has happened at the college. The finance office says it's against their policy to refund any of our money. We are both in shock. I tell Christie not to worry. We will write a letter to the president of the school and tell her our financial situation. We will be brutally honest. It's embarrassing to admit our financial struggles, but this is too much money for us to just let go. She will understand and refund something, if not the entire amount. He was only at school a few weeks. We send a heartfelt letter to the President, of course mentioning that I'm an alumni.

A few weeks later she responds. Sorry, we just don't give refunds for this type of situation. I'm flabbergasted. Disgusted might be a better word. They are dripping in money. It's obvious. They just built a $40 million dollar student center. This school has had a special place in my heart for over thirty years. I always have wonderful things to say about it. It was one of the best learning experiences in my life.

Maybe when the leadership changes I will feel good about the school again. I can't knock them for making YHC a bigger and better place. The campus is amazing. The school has grown and attracted students from all across the United States. Obviously I wanted my son to attend. I can knock the leadership for needing to think a bit more deeply about students who get in trouble and how to handle them. It's not a thoughtful policy. In fact, it stinks. I'm kicking myself for telling Christie to go ahead and pay the entire amount. We actually had a thoughtful discussion on it before we wrote the check. I now wish we had set up a monthly payment plan. But we didn't.

After three months, my friend lets me go from his company. We agree it's not working. I manage a few meetings but no sales. I burned some bridges, so it's not easy. Hell, I didn't just burn bridges. When they were on fire, I tossed a few grenades on them. Some people ignore my calls altogether. I would probably do the same. It doesn't matter, though. I've proven to myself that I can handle corporate meetings and all the bullshit stuff that goes with them. Not that I want to, but I can.

Christie gets laid off from her job less than a week after I do. She has been working there for six months, a giant healthcare management company. She gets fired on a Friday. Payday. They have a meeting first thing in the morning. Her boss's boss and a Human Resources robot are present. She needs to leave the office immediately. Take all your belongings and go. She is escorted out of the office by the HR robot. He also mentions that today will be her last paycheck. No severance. Not even two weeks pay. This company is a billion-dollar behemoth. She is in shock. She calls me on the way home in tears. I'm in shock too, for a different reason. Both of us got fired in the same week. What are the odds?

Chapter 38

September-October 2014

    I tell Christie we will figure something out. I have an idea.

    Christie has a plan too. She's pissed by the time she gets home. The tears are dry. She wants that two weeks severance. Those bastards. How dare they! She will use one very simple tool to get what she wants: the truth. She sends a letter to the human resources director (not the robot from her meeting) and explains that she was never given a single negative performance review. She shouldn't have been let go without having a chance to improve things if management was having issues. She essentially makes her boss look like the incompetent manager she is. The letter works. They don't want to make it a big deal. She gets the two weeks.

    Her anger kind of turns me on. I love her passion around this injustice. It's sexy when a woman stands up for herself. We have sex that night. Angry, I-just-got-fired sex. For some reason, she punches me in the head when she comes. For some reason, this turns me on and I come too. Sex is funny.

Why is this story important? Not the sex, the other parts?

Tom got fired. Christie got fired. Austin got kicked out of college. All in less than a month.

Christie is crushed. Austin is stoned. I'm feeling ...O.K. Hell, I shouldn't even be alive. But I am. I clawed my way back from madness. I have my wits about me. The executive function of my brain is working again. We can fix this. I can fix this. Don't get me wrong, I'm very concerned about Austin's drug use. I also know there is nothing I can really do without money and without his desire to get help.

I have a plan: Start a new business. It worked before. Not an advertising agency. A marketing consulting company. Why not? I've done this shit for twenty years. There is no part of marketing that I don't thoroughly understand. I've worked with nearly every vertical industry. I know me some marketing. I've got my confidence back. I tell her my plan. Let's start a consulting company. I can make this work again, but I need your help. You like to do the work that I don't. It makes sense. Think about it. We did it before. We can do it again. Fuck our bad luck. Let's make luck our bitch. Make her do our bidding.

I can tell Christie is interested.

The Mattes are getting their mojo back!

We start Revolve Marketing, a consulting agency. I'm the marketing and creative consultant. Christie will handle the business side. She also wants control over the company finances, just to be safe. It's a smart move.

We need to borrow money from Christie's dad to get us started.

We have mojo but still don't have any money.

Chapter 39

November 2014-May 2015

I write my second email looking for a research partner, this one to the Allen Brain Institute in California. I also leave a message with the public relations contact. I never hear back.

My third email, a month later, is to the M.I.T neuroscience department. They also don't respond. I'm not sure what to do now. I thought someone would be interested in researching my brain at this point. I guess not. Maybe they don't believe me. Who knows? I decide to focus on work for the next year. Revolve needs clients. The money we borrowed from Christie's dad won't last long.

It has been six months. I'm back in front of the Hall County judge. I get an all-good from my probation officer. Another congratulations from the judge. This actually makes me feel good. I like this lady. I know my life is moving in the right direction. Because my home is in Johns Creek, my probation is now transferred to the City of Atlanta probation system. This bothers me because I really like my probation officer. I feel a connection to him. It feels like he also wants me to succeed. He tells me I'm one of the only guys he's worked with who's this conscientious. Good to know.

I check in with the probation center in Southwest Atlanta. It's just a little shorter ride from my home than Hall County, but in the other direction. Oh, well. I get placed in the system and meet with an officer for ten minutes. He is not my assigned probation officer. I have no assigned probation officer, he tells me. On the paperwork, where the form says Probation Officer, someone has filled in: Atlanta SW probation. That's it. No officer name. The good news is that I just have to call in every month and answer a series of questions. This is a big relief. I don't have to make the hour drive to Southwest Atlanta every month. It's a big win for convenience. I still have some court fees to pay. I can do those over time. I will be on probation for another four years.

Christie and I may be doing better, but Austin is still struggling. He gets in a car wreck sometime around Thanksgiving. He damages some property with the car and leaves the scene. Bad move. The Johns Creek prosecutor wants him to spend the weekend in jail. Christie decides to hire a lawyer and have it moved to Fulton County. The lawyer thinks she will be able to get a better plea deal. She does. Austin doesn't have to spend any time in jail. He does have community service. Lots of it.

Christie goes to lunch with a former colleague, a PR professional who has a potential new client with some marketing needs. We decide to pitch it as a team. Together we win the account. We start to work on a new creative campaign. It feels good to be creating and presenting ideas again. Selling the creative rationale and concepts to a new client. I forgot how much I love the show. They keep us busy for a year. Slowly, Christie and I start making a little money.

Austin is working as a waiter in a local restaurant. This is not the future we envisioned for him when he was growing up. More importantly, this is not the life he wants. Waiting tables isn't the issue. I waited tables. Lots of people wait tables. He is adrift. It's apparent to both of us. We know he's using something. Thank God he's not getting into any trouble. He stays on the bottom floor of our townhome, hanging out. He reminds me of myself when I used to hide in the guest room of our old house. He works a few shifts a week. He's not happy. It's obvious to all of us. I tell Christie we need to get him in rehab as soon as we have money. He won't go to AA meetings either. He doesn't understand how helpful they can be. He says they're stupid.

Carson is excelling in his musical theater classes. He's decided this will be his college major. He has a lot of work ahead over the next year applying to the best musical theater programs in the country. The best analogy would be to compare it with college football recruitment. The best football colleges want the best players. Carson's good enough to make a number of programs. The colleges all want different types of performers and players, a perfect mix of talent for an entertaining season. He just needs to decide on the right program.

In April he performs on stage at a local theater in the role of Kerchak, from the *Tarzan* musical. Kerchak is the ape father of Tarzan. I hardly recognize him when he comes on stage. As soon as he starts to sing, I know it's him. It's a great show. He shines. All the kids do.

Our kids are traveling their own paths. We want to help them as much as we can, but a parent can only do so much. Our children have their own journeys.

Christie and I are in a meeting with the new client and my phone vibrates. It's a text from the JCS probation office. I need to report in two days. This is not a good sign. My monthly probation meeting is not for another ten days. I start to panic – come to find out, for a good reason. There is a petition for a modification of probation/revocation of probation report. It claims I am in willful disregard of my court order, specifically the following:

Condition 11: failed to pay restitution totaling $48,456,57 and currently has an outstanding balance of $44,923.57 to City of Johns Creek

They want to send me to jail for being broke. This is too much for me to deal with. Christie and I are just getting back on our feet. This year has been good. Blessings are coming our way. We have some money now – enough to make our monthly nut, but nothing close to my outstanding balance. I wish I could say that I was pissed. I'll show these assholes! They can't pick on me anymore. I've started a new business. I'm not mentally ill now. I'm a new man. But I'm not pissed. I'm scared. I don't want to go to jail again. I've come so far. The judge can do whatever he feels like. If I get the prosecutor from 2013, I'm screwed.

I do what any intelligent non-psychotic person with some money would do. I call a lawyer. A criminal defense lawyer who handles DUI's and multiple DUI cases. My charges are traffic charges, misdemeanors. But I'm not taking any chances. I want the best. I find him, an Atlanta lawyer named Kevin F. Christie and I meet in his office for an hour. He decides to take my case. The cost is $3,500. It includes all the paperwork, research, and two trips to the courthouse in Johns Creek if needed. I can't sign the agreement fast enough. He also can't guarantee the outcome. He promises to get to the bottom of the confusion and miscommunication with State Farm. Find out why they decided to revoke the probation. He looks at all my other conditions of probation. He asks if I did the drug evaluation. I tell him yes. Years ago. I gave the letter to JCS. The probation company. They have it on file. Let's not take any chances, he says. Let's do another one. It may help with the decision. Fine by me.

    I report to a clinical alcohol/drug evaluation center. I spend a long time with the drug counselor. He asks lots of questions. I'm not sure what to expect at the end. He sends a report over to my attorney. It's a few pages with my history. The important part for me is the last few lines. The summation:

    Diagnosis: No symptoms/impairment uncovered
    Prognosis: Non-Problematic
    Considering all the profile characteristics no treatment is recommended.

    Excellent news. Kevin has also talked to the courthouse. State Farm has in fact paid them some money. Just like I've been saying. The only problem, it's not enough to cover the price of a new police car. He asks me how much money can I get. Maybe $8,000. That's not going to be enough, he says. They want $20,000, and if the judge and prosecutor can agree, you will also be off probation. Finished with everything. I tell him I'll see what I can do. I call my sister and tell her the court is going to send me back to jail if I can't pay my restitution. She has been my toughest critic in the past. Understandably, pissed at all the shit I've done to my family. She has also seen how far I've come. She tells me she will loan me $15,000. She saves me. I thank her and hang up. I call Kevin back and tell him I can be in court with a certified check for $16,000. That really is all the money I can get, and I have to borrow it. I ask him to remind the court that I have kids and I'm getting back on my feet. Tell them I have a new consulting company. If I go to jail, I will lose any possibility of getting the money. He calls me back the next day and says we probably have a deal. Still no guarantees. Meet me at Johns Creek the morning of May 14 with the certified check. We will talk to the judge and the prosecutor.

On the morning of my court date, I arrive on time, check in hand. I feel like I'm going to puke. Kevin said it would be the last item of the day on the judge's docket. I listen to all the other traffic cases. One guy gets handcuffed for some reason. I feel his pain. I'm not really listening. A bunch of cops are gathered outside the courtroom window looking inside. They are milling about in the hallway. I'm wondering if they know who I am. They must know. None of them look like the officers who came in to look at the madman from three years ago. I don't know if they are staring me down or just talking to each other. I mean, it's a police station. You're going to see a policeman or two. I think about how far I've come. I feel no ill will toward any of these guys. I never have. Maybe I did at one time, for like an hour, on a day when I was out of my mind. But that was so long ago and I was wrong. I want to apologize to all of them. It's probably not a good idea. They may still be pissed at me for the cop car incident. I just don't know. Hurry up, Kevin. I need this to be over.

Kevin arrives in good spirits. He tells me to sit tight. He has another client he needs to handle first. Finally my case comes up. Kevin calls me to the back offices to meet the prosecutor. I've never seen him before. He looks a bit like Louis C.K., the comedian. He gives off a good vibe. He smiles too. A good sign. We shake hands and he tells me we have a deal. Let's go get the judge to sign the papers.

I'm floating. We walk to the judge's desk. The court is empty now except for us. This is the same judge who originally sentenced me in January 2012. He shows no malice toward me at all. He didn't back then either. I'm not sure what he's thinking. He can see I look different. I'm certainly acting different. Then he does it. He signs my release. Probation terminated upon receipt of a check for $16,000 as agreed by the city.

I'm beaming as I walk to my car. I can't thank Kevin enough. As far as I'm concerned, he did the impossible. I feel so good I ask him if the cops still hate me. I can handle the answer, the truth. He doesn't answer. He just says cops stick together. Then he asks a question of his own: When all this was going on, did you spend some time in the islands? A few people inside seem to think so. I've told Kevin the condensed story with regard to my actions over the last few years. He knows about the crazy. I remind him that I did spend some time in St John.

I guess they came after me so hard because they thought I could pay the money. They thought I was wealthy. I was wealthy for much of the time I lived in Johns Creek. If not exactly wealthy, I certainly had money. Or I could get it. Now? Not so much.

I'm not going to jail. This is a great day.

Future Life

Chapter 40

June-December 2015

    Christie notices a shirt missing from her closet. She can't find it anywhere. A favorite pair of shoes are gone too. She asks me if I've seen them. No. I tell her she might want to check Austin's closet. He could be stealing your clothes and selling them to a consignment shop. If his addiction is getting this bad, there is no telling what he will do.

    She goes downstairs and looks through his closet. She finds an old blouse that the store must not have been interested in buying. When he gets home from work, we confront him. He denies it. We know better. I tell Christie not to panic, but I can see in her eyes she's terrified. It's one thing to have a husband with addiction issues, but when it's your child it's something else entirely. It's paralyzing. She starts researching recovery centers in the South. It doesn't make the situation any less terrifying but at least she's taking action. Austin has always been headstrong, outspoken, and persistent. All characteristics we thought would make him unstoppable in this world. As parents, we always assumed he would go to college and excel at it. With his ability to debate and not give up on an argument, we thought maybe he'd be a lawyer or a politician. To say we were disappointed when he was kicked out of college would be an understatement. You always want to see your child happy and following their passions. But when you realize your child is an addict, just keeping him alive is enough. Christie finds a rehab facility in Georgia. One that looks right for Austin. He refuses to go.

The next week money is missing from Christie's checking account. A few hundred dollars. We are about to confront Austin when Christie gets a text from one of his old friends. She hasn't seen Austin in a while, but she's heard through the grapevine that he's using heroin. She wants us to know. We thank her for the text. We need to do something now. We walk into his bedroom. He's white, like a ghost. He's slurring his words. Today is the day we panic. We thought it was getting worse, but we had no idea it was this bad. We tell him he's going to rehab today. If he doesn't go now, we are calling the police and having him arrested for stealing. He agrees to go. He knows it's out of control. We get to the recovery center and start the admission process. It takes some time, Austin is starting to detox when we leave. I know he has a few tough days ahead. This place will help make it bearable. On the drive home we feel relieved. Austin is safe. We'll take what we can and be thankful.

None of the recovery centers take our insurance. We need to borrow money. Again. It's to save our son's life. We have no trouble asking this time.

We get to see Austin two weeks after his admission. We spend a few hours with him on a Sunday. He looks better. His face glows. He's smiling again. We are slowly watching our son come back to life. After thirty-five days, we decide as a family to continue his rehab in Charleston, South Carolina. His counselor advises us it takes more than thirty-five days to make this work. I know this to be true. He needs to live in the solution for a while before stepping back into the real world. We drive him to Charleston the weekend of a historic flood. Roads are flooded and businesses are closing. We keep driving. When we arrive at the house, everyone is waiting outside in the pouring rain and four inches of standing water. Every person is there waiting to welcome our son. We say our goodbyes and are hopeful this place will make a difference. He's safe for at least another ninety days.

Christie and I love everything fall, the cooler weather, Halloween, wearing sweaters, celebrating our birthdays and going to fall festivals. It's been stressful over the past few months, so we need a break. A night to laugh and forget about our many worries. Every October the city of Cumming, Georgia, has a huge fall fair. We arrive at dusk. Beautiful sunset. We take some pictures and post them on Facebook. It's a great night. The rides. The games. We see a psychic. She tells us good things are in our future. Money too. I'm down with that.

While we're walking through the crowds of people, something fascinating happens. Occasionally when I make eye contact with someone, I see a soft colored light bounce off their eyes. All colors: red, orange, yellow, green, blue, indigo, and violet. Depending on the person, the color changes. It's so fast that I almost don't notice it. But I do notice it. It's one hundred times faster than a lightning bugs flash. I may have seen this before, but I ignored it. Or I thought it was just a ... I don't know what. I just ignored it.

This night I can't ignore it. It happens over and over again. The age or sex of the person doesn't seem to matter. Young or old. Male or female. Neither does the race or eye color. In fact, I don't even need to make eye contact. I can be looking at their eyes and they can be looking at something or someone else. With all the wild things my brain has done, this one is totally new. I have no idea what the colors mean. I never know when it's going to happen. It just does.

A few weeks later, Christie and I watch one of the X-Men movies on HBO. After it's over, I wonder out loud, "You know I could be some kind of mutant. It's possible."

She gives me a huge eye roll. "I don't think being an addict or psychotic qualifies as genetic mutations."

"Maybe not, but they have genetic components. Maybe all the drugs I've done turned something on in my brain, at the genetic level. Just think about it for a second!"

I get another eye roll, and this time she adds a dramatic pause to let me know just how absurd I sound. "So you think you're a mutant? Like an X-Man? Great, just my luck! I was married to an X-Man! Except I got *Tom, The Man With Upsight* instead of Hugh Jackman."

I smile a little and keep talking. "Or, what if I'm more like Spiderman? Spiderman isn't an X-Man. He got his powers after being bitten by a radioactive spider, not from a genetic mutation. When Spiderman got his *spidey senses*, it took him a while to learn how to use them. Maybe I've been getting used to my new senses. Getting used to having and using my Upsight."

She's laughing now. "So let me get this straight: In this new scenario, you're a fifty-year-old man using radioactive coke instead of a teenage comic book character who was bitten by a radioactive spider? Are you freaking high? So does Upsight come from a genetic mutation or radioactive cocaine?"

"Maybe it's a little of both," I answer. "I did so many drugs that I upregulated a gene in my DNA."

"I have no idea what upregulated means."

"It's an increase in cellular connections or activity due to external input. Or something like that.

Christie looks at me thoughtfully. "So, you're suggesting that you did so much cocaine that you turned on some genes in your DNA and this mutation is the reason you're having these visions?"

"Yeah. Maybe."

"OK, I get your argument," Christie says, "but you might want to do a little more research. You're not an X-Man. And you don't have accidental superpowers."

As much as I like spending time trying to figure how and why my mind is changing, it's not exactly profitable. Our consulting company has active projects, but as a salesman, I know there always has to be work in the pipeline. I look through my contacts and come across an old friend, Tom H. I haven't seen him in over twenty-five years. He runs a small independent film and video production company in Atlanta. He's been in business for thirty years and his company is growing and changing with the times. Photography, corporate videos, and a studio production facility. He's the whole package. Building Atlanta's reputation as the Hollywood of the South.

I shoot him an email and ask him to lunch. He says he'd love to get together. We set a date. I want to catch up on his life and discuss the possibilities of doing marketing for his studio. They don't have a large social media presence. No real marketing at all to speak of. I drive to his studio and get a quick tour. We talk about how much the movie industry is changing in Atlanta. His company is always busy. It's an exciting time; he's making a shift from corporate films to independent movies. His first low-budget horror movie will be coming out in March. I congratulate him on his success. We decide on a Cuban restaurant near his studio for lunch. On the walk over, I start thinking about what I can do to market his horror movie. This might be a good fit. I love horror movies.

Before we talk business, we need to catch up on life. It's been a long time. I tell him how I lost everything in a drug-fueled psychotic breakdown. He wants details. So I share a few of my adventures. Christie's porn empire, the T-boned cop car, the Beverly Hills Hotel break-in, the psych ward, even the aliens. He is wide-eyed at some points. Laughing really hard at other times. I'm lost in the memories and just keep talking. He finally stops me mid-sentence and says, "Are you pitching me?"

I'm caught off guard. "What do you mean?"

"Are you trying to sell me a movie idea? Your story is reality gold. People love this shit. They would go see your movie and thank God their lives are not as screwed-up as yours. It would make people feel better about their problems. After the movie, couples will go grab a drink and discuss your shitty-ass life."

I'm not sure how to respond to his comment. Thank you seems a bit strange.

I finally settle on, "No kidding."

On the walk back to his studio, I tell him about Upsight and my visions. How incredible they are and how I can access them anytime.

He says, "It sounds like your brain is receiving the deluxe cable package and the rest of us are getting basic cable."

Holy shit! This is the perfect metaphor. That is exactly what it feels like. Before I lost my mind, I was getting the basic cable package. Now I'm getting the deluxe cable package. The only problem is that I'm receiving some Telemundo-type channels and I don't speak Spanish. I'm also getting the Math Channel, the Physics Channel, and the Hallucinations Channel.

The question is: Where are the new signals coming from? What part of my brain is broadcasting these messages? What part of my brain is picking them up?

As I'm leaving, he suggests writing about my experiences. I tell him I'm not a writer. He says no problem, just outline everything with bullet points and they'll find someone who can write the movie script and who knows, it may get the attention of a university researcher. I tell him I'll think about it. We leave with a handshake and no firm plans on another meeting. I don't bring up marketing his horror movie. He's got me thinking about too many other things.

Tom Matte

Chapter 41

January-December 2016

On January 6, I start writing. It's supposed to be the outline for a movie script. I can't do it, just an outline. It's not that simple. I've got too much to say. I text Tom and tell him that his outline idea is turning into an actual book. A memoir. I'll get back to him when I'm finished.

Since I'm in a writing mode, I decide to send another email to the neuroscientist, Stanislas Dehaene. He has written a book called *Consciousness and the Brain: Deciphering How The Brain Codes Our Thoughts*. He researches and writes about many of the same things I'm studying. Most importantly, he thinks about consciousness as a network. That's good, because from what I see, it is a network.

My email is over seven pages. I go into great detail about my abilities and the need to find out what's happening to my brain when I'm accessing my visions. I know I can reproduce these visions in a lab. I just want someone to measure them.

I never hear back. No surprise. I'm used to it. One trait that I haven't lost is persistence.

I know that if I could find one amazing mathematical discovery using the gift of Upsight, then researchers would have to take notice. But so far nothing I've found would be considered groundbreaking. Hopefully that will change soon.

The act of writing gives me time to reflect. If nothing else, it's a cathartic process. Reflecting on the past gives the present a new perspective.

A good friend asked me why I was writing this book. What do I want people to take away from reading it? I told her, first, I want them to be entertained. Second, but as important, I hope it gets the attention of academic researchers. I want this book to be the spark that gets others as interested in Upsight as I am. I know something has changed in my brain. Let's figure out what it is. Could it be a key to help other people with mental illness and addiction issues? I'd like to think so. I believe it is.

Carson is a senior this year. He and Christie have been researching and traveling across the country touring colleges for most of the year. It's a different process when you're applying to musical theater programs. You apply, then audition, and hope to get an offer from a well-respected program. Most programs only have spots for twelve new musical theater students each year. He is fortunate. He has multiple scholarship offers. It's an exciting time for him.

He's on a roll. He's cast as Jimmy in the musical *Thoroughly Modern Millie*. This will be his last community show before he leaves for college. The entire cast hits a home run with their performances. Closing night is a bittersweet moment. The next time we will see him onstage will be in a college production. It could be a while. Freshmen don't always get parts their first year. We don't want to wait that long. Between high school and local theater, we're spoiled watching him perform every few months.

After much deliberation he settles on Coastal Carolina University in Myrtle Beach, South Carolina. He loves the vibe of the school. He says they're his people. Christie and I are elated. It's only five hours from home. Far enough away for him and close enough for us to drive and watch his performances.

He graduates from high school on May 26, 2016.

Austin leaves rehab before his ninety days are finished. It was around the holidays, so we agreed to take him out a few days early. He looks like a different person. This is the kid who used to make us laugh and frustrate us to no end when he was growing up. Except he's not a kid anymore. He's a young man. He is accepting responsibility for his actions now. Hallelujah! He starts thinking about his future. The sky's the limit. He doesn't think AA is stupid anymore. We're excited to have him home but realize it may not be the best place for him. It's hard to step back into your old life like nothing ever happened.

He has a short relapse but quickly gets back on track. He decides on his own to head back to Charleston to live with his peers in recovery. This time, Christie and I get to see him graduate from his recovery program after ninety days. He has almost seven months of total clean time. This is a big deal. He can live without drugs and be happy.

At his commencement, we listen to friends tell stories about how helpful he is in the morning making breakfast.

How he is always there when someone needs a kind word. How funny and quick-witted he is. Person after person, sharing what he has meant to their own recovery. It's almost like they're talking about someone else. But we know, he's always been that kid. When he was younger, he was the first one to try something new, the first one to stick up for a friend, and the first one to tell you he loved you. We are beaming with pride. The past few years tore his world apart, but it's clear that he is ready to move on.

Austin and some of his recovery friends come spend time with us in Atlanta. We have some great laughs. We even talk about "when dad was crazy." Enough time has passed and the wounds are healing. I feel his love for me again. It feels great. I don't want to do anything to jeopardize it. His love is too precious. All love is.

Occasionally I still wake up in the middle of the night wondering if I've scarred them for life. Ruined their future relationships or their ability to trust. So everyday I make sure I'm present and they know how much they are loved. That's all I know how to do.

I have Christie to thank for holding their world together. Not just their world but mine too. She took the brunt of my crazy and shielded them the best she could. She didn't shield them because she loved me; she did it because she loved them more than she hated me. She did it because she hoped that one day our relationship would be reparable. I know there are those who think she's insane for letting me back into her life. Her friends, her family, most likely even she thinks it at times. But why? Why did she let me back in? I like to think it's because she knew me as her best friend first, as a good husband, a logical business partner, and a loving dad. I remember not long after I came back, Austin told her she was stupid for letting me back into their lives. She was crushed. She thought she was letting him down. I told her one day that because of her, our kids would look back on this time as a lesson of love and forgiveness and not bitterness and hate. I'm lucky, I know. Her heart is her family. Mine is too. I'd say we are definitely a family again. Maybe a little bruised and battered. But also a little wiser. A lot more thankful for each normal day. OK, with us normal may be a stretch. So I'll say thankful for each new day we are together.

It has taken years, but finally I don't hate myself for causing so much pain to the people I love the most. Myself included. My family forgives me for the suffering I caused them. I know because they've told me. Forgiveness is powerful. It works miracles. I've learned something from every mistake. Some things I didn't want to learn. Some I had to learn. And some I'm still learning.

I was lost for 2012 and 2013. Literally and figuratively. I was a wanderer. Drifting from place to place.

Am I the only one? Not by a long shot. The lost and lonely are everywhere.

Am I lucky? Definitely! Of course I had some help. Along the way there were Angels and Aliens at every turn.

Looking back now, it feels like they were all put there for a reason. They were beacons of light in the dark. Living lights. Everyone I've met on my journey has been pointing me in one direction.

Home.

THE END

Afterword

Christie has some final words.

I've been asked a thousand times: *How did I get through it?*

When people hear Tom's story--our story really, even my condensed conversational version--nine times out of 10 their responses can be summed up in these three reactions:

"I can't believe how strong you are."

"I can't believe your family survived."

"I can't believe you stayed together."

Since you've reached the end of Tom's memoir, you might be thinking the same thing, or something close.

I have spent years trying to figure out how we moved past the craziness, addiction, mental illness, and hurt, but every answer sounded like a mantra from a self-help book in my head – blah, blah, blah. Those books can be great, but they've never been my thing. So eventually I stopped trying to figure out the "how" and focused on the "what."

Here's what I've learned.

I've learned that I'm strong, but so are most of the people I know. We lived in a perfect bubble and believe me, over the last 10 years there are many times I wish I still got my mail there. But when you're in a bubble it's hard to be open and vulnerable. Once the word gets out that your husband was playing smash-up derby with a cop car because he thought you were a porn star, all bets are off and your life is out in the open. But during that time, I also found that because I was vulnerable, my friends and even strangers opened up about their own struggles. In a way became a safe space for others, and in doing so their stories showed me that everyone possesses amazing strength given the right opportunity.

I learned that our family could survive. We were fortunate; friends and family circled the wagons and helped us breathe. I was numb, but someone gave me a list of three things to do every day. Wake up and put your feet on the ground. Make up your bed. Take a shower. That seemed doable. At least it was a start. I took that simple list to heart until one day I started adding normal things back on the to-do list. I also made sure my kids knew two things: that we were going to be OK and that they were loved. I also didn't trash their dad (yes, I know I'm a saint), but up until the time he took a swan dive off the deep end, he was a good father. They had to learn to navigate this shitty situation, and thankfully they came out the other side better human beings. We survived. I include Tom in that "we."

I learned we were better together. This one was tricky. But remember, we went from friends, to friends with benefits, to parents, to husband and wife, to divorced, to "it's complicated." But you know what? In truth, our relationship has always been complicated, in good ways and in weird ways; in joyous ways and sometimes in really difficult ways. At the end of the day, taken altogether, I love that about us. I wouldn't choose to do life with anyone else, and I'm grateful every day that our story has as much healing and forgiveness as it has had devastation. (I'm also deeply aware that many addiction and mental illness stories don't end this way; that many of them can't and shouldn't.)

What it boils down to: Even though our lives for a time were made up of days that were stranger than fiction, we learned from them. Would I want to relive any of those days? Hell no! But we are stronger, better human beings because of them.

About The Author

Photo: Nat Carter, Artography

Tom Matte, originally from Upstate New York, has called Atlanta his home for over 30 years. He works with mental health marketers offering marketing strategy and insights into connecting with individuals or families going through a mental health crisis. He also tells his story through speaking engagements, interviews, and the written word. He thinks different-because he sees different.